Lessons from CLOD

An Inspiring Story of Art, Philanthropy and Entrepreneurship

HAL HANSON, M.D.

For more information on Artist Jeff Hanson, his original commissioned artwork, speaking engagements or to contact the author: www.JeffreyOwenHanson.com

Artist's Premium Hardcover Edition:
ISBN 13: 978-0-9883842-0-0   ISBN 10: 0988384205
Library of Congress Control Number: 2013902986

Standard Hardcover Edition:
ISBN 13: 978-0-9883842-1-7   ISBN 10: 0988384213
Library of Congress Control Number: 20130903923

Library of Congress Cataloging-in Publication Data on file with publisher.

Published by Harold Hanson

Printed in the United States of America

 Book Designed By: Jennifer Bedell, JJB Creative Design, LLC
www.jjbcreativedesign.com

For Jeffrey

CONTENTS

INTRODUCTION

This book represents where I have been for the past seven years. No…not writing it. **Living it!**

As an emergency room physician, I have no formal training in writing or storytelling. I apologize for my incomplete sentences, changes of tense, stream of consciousness style and grammatical errors. My sixth-grade teacher back in Iowa, Hazel Appenzeller, would cringe.

And I have no sensational life-story of my own. My entire career has been very predictable. Sure, I have anecdotes from the ER, but they are just brief encounters and events. None that couldn't be summed up in a couple of paragraphs.

But I do have one great story to tell. An amazing, meandering true story, very close to me, that I really must share.

Jeffrey Owen Hanson. Now **HE** has a story! An over-the-top story. And I am not just saying that because I am his father. At first I didn't realize how wonderful the story was, because I was too close to it. And it was too painful. I had lived it with him, day to day, along with his mother, Julie, as it unfolded. Emotionally imbedded in all the heartbreak and all the tears, all the surprises, achievements and accolades, it was just impossible to step back and objectively analyze the entire circumstance. But as people around us have repeatedly pointed out, Jeff's journey through adversity, becoming defined by generosity, his success in the art world and his award-winning entrepreneurship comprise a story that movie makers and playwrights dream to capture even once in a lifetime. I only hope I have served it justice, to tell it as it occurred, and allow the reader to draw their own conclusions.

I have struggled to title this book. And those close to the journey have offered many alternative suggestions. Many of the chapter titles would work, but none of them really sum it up. The final choice was Jeff's.

The contents of the book are divided into four sections. RECOLLECTIONS relate an amazing sequence of events occurring between 2005 and 2012. OBSERVATIONS are an interlude from the story line and could arguably be moved to the end of the book, as an appendix. But they are instead offered after RECOLLECTIONS as a colorful pause for self-examination and discovery—an intermission to look at where we are and how we got here, before moving toward HORIZONS for our future. LESSONS summarize the journey and offer some takeaways to apply to our own lives.

I chuckle to myself as I comb through our endless family photographs, baby books, home videos, newspaper and magazine clippings, TV news spots, trophies, awards, school papers, letters, emails and diaries. As two "type-A, OCD, anal (*and proud of it*)" parents of an only child, we have documented and chronicled Jeff's childhood to the "nth" degree. The poor kid has had a camera in his face his entire life. But we would have recorded his life just the same, even if he didn't have a great story. Thank you, OCD! You sure helped me create this manuscript.

Friends who knew I was writing this, through 2012, have often asked me, "What is this book about?" I honestly don't have a quick answer. I could say it is "Jeff's biography" (to the ripe old age of 19), but that sounds hokey and misses the message. And the message itself is not so simple to verbalize, either. Woven into the story are life lessons that gradually became understood by the three of us making the journey together. Unspoken lessons that became very important to us, and shaped the way we now think and live. And the best part is, unlike so many books and movies, the journey is not over yet. The story continues, and really has no ending in sight. Maybe fodder for a sequel.

"Goosebumps, tears and smiles." Julie says every great book, play or movie must have all three components to make it memorable and successful. Our son Jeffrey's story has them all. God bless you, Jeff. Read on.

Hal Hanson
Kansas City, March 2013

Jeff H. 1

RECOLLECTIONS

A Medical Story

You don't let go of your dreams all at once...it happens slowly. They drift away gradually...in small increments. You start with a **bank of dreams**, goals and aspirations. The American dream for your child. It's just assumed. Taken for granted. A normal, perfect baby that meets all the developmental milestones in record time. The best soccer player on the team. Honor student. Lead role in the school musical. Quarterback of the football team. College at Harvard. Ph.D. in nuclear physics. Astronaut, and then President of the United States and Microsoft, simultaneously!

But events start chipping away at your dreams. And you have to lower your expectations...just a little at first...it's too painful to let go of too much at once.

(**Neu′ ro fi bro ma to′sis**) a genetic, familial condition characterized by developmental changes in the nervous system, muscles, bones and skin. Associated with developmental delays, learning disabilities, ADHD, pigmented spots on the skin, skin lumps or fibromas, and rarely, optic nerve tumors.

Deceptively angelic in these early photos,
Jeffrey Owen Hanson was the usual busy toddler.
Although there was no formal diagnosis of
neurofibromatosis type I until age six, Jeff
had some of the hallmark café au lait skin
spots from birth.

No one in our family has this. How can this be?

Jeffrey Owen Hanson, age six, our only child, future Apple CEO, Warren Buffett's choice as his successor at Berkshire Hathaway and Olympic gold medalist in gymnastics...HAS WHAT?!

Silently, a few dreams float out the window.

Speech therapy. School meetings. IQ testing. IEP's. Medication for ADHD? NO WAY! The stigma of "needing medications." And having to take them at school? People will find out...our baby is not...(quite)...perfect.

Another withdrawal from our dream bank.

A funny little gimp in Jeff's gait, a quirky slow style of running. An unusual inflection in his speech. A left thumb that liked to posture itself in extension. A left arm that was often ignored, never wanting to help the right arm with any task. Jeff pushed his peas around on his plate, right-handed, never capturing them. Lefty just hung down at his side, neglected.

Restless, hyperactive days—sleepless nights. No one rested. All apparent manifestations of neurofibromatosis.

Events kept chipping away at my dreams.

(Op´tic Gli o´ma) a slow-growing tumor of neuroglial tissue in an optic nerve or optic chiasm, heralded by visual loss. Associated with neurofibromatosis Type I.

Slow growing? That didn't console me. Jeff had a pea-sized tumor, *optic glioma*, found on MRI in his optic chiasm, where his two optic nerves cross before they enter his eye balls. "May not" cause a vision problem. Needs to be watched. Track with quarterly brain MRI's, under sedation, and vision monitoring. Probably OK. Life can go on as usual.

But...good-bye astronaut, microbiologist, airline pilot and sharp shooter. ("Jeff for President" is still OK).

A few more dreams drift away.

The new bicycle. Every kid can ride a bicycle. Jeff didn't exactly pick up on it right away, like the neighbor kids. So, with training wheels mounted, we peddled up and down the sidewalk, Dad jogging along side. Until the training wheels wore out. They must have been "cheap." But Jeff couldn't ride without them. Another set mounted, which gradually wore to the rim the next summer. And by then, the novelty of the "new bike" had worn off. It was too much work to peddle, and there was no balance to ride independently.

The bicycle dream went to the garage sale.

And while other elementary children were roller-skating around us, zipping by at high speed, we clung to the railing around the perimeter of the rink. Poor balance? Keep practicing. And practicing. And practicing. Until after two years of after-school skating parties, we just attended, put on our skates, sat on the benches and ate snacks. Jeff couldn't skate at all. Did anyone notice? Was he lost in the crowd? It just got easier not to attend anymore. So he didn't.

Vision began slipping...subtle, at first. It's hard to tell what a ten-year-old sees. But little things became apparent. Reading "he" instead of "the," "here" instead of "there," "23" instead of "423," even with glasses on. Jeff couldn't see the characters to the left of his visual midline. (Try getting your math worksheet correct when you never see the first number).

Reading became increasingly difficult. Jeff's chair was moving gradually closer to the TV and computer. Frustration with hand-held games. Couldn't catch a ball. Bumping the shopping cart into

Jeff was always right there in the kitchen when the mixer came out. Jeff is the alien on the left, Hal on the right, communicating the universal peace greeting. Theodore Edward Bear, "bearly" tolerating his annoying brother, Jeff, circa 1995. We always seemed to be out of shaving cream.

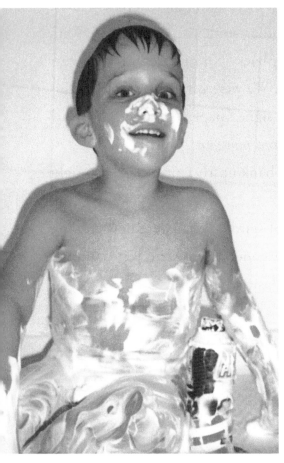

anyone approaching from the left. Walking off curbs. Falling down stairs. Unable to play ping pong anymore. Couldn't use the sight on the BB gun. And then, the Nintendo GameBoy DS—Jeff's most coveted possession that he had saved money for—Jeff gave it away! He just couldn't see the animation on the screens anymore. Vision was failing.

I shudder at the number of dreams that left me.

It was at a sixth grade IEP (individual educational plan) meeting with teachers, counselors and the principal that I started to recognize the magnitude of the problem. The topic was math. Between learning disabilities and vision problems, the decision was made to stop trying to stay on "grade level" any longer. It was impossible. The school would just continue teaching basic math as best they could at a slower pace, and Jeff would not be at sixth grade level anymore. He wouldn't take math with the other students. Or reading. With this decision, there was no turning back. No catching up next year. No more "main stream" education. We were officially declaring this would be a "child left behind." We signed papers, giving our permission. *Just learn what you can, Jeff, and move on.*

My heart pounded as my dream bank nearly emptied itself—right out the principal's window.

And these weren't just dreams of stardom that were now stealing away. No, those were already long gone. These were just common ordinary activities of daily living. Basic stuff.

Slowly chipping away.

Jeff had never seen my old telescope packed away in our basement. A hobby of mine, pre-Jeff. Boxed away for a dozen years, I took it out and assembled it, thinking the magnification would allow Jeff to see the moon and stars more clearly. We stood on the patio behind our house, and gazed up at the sky. It was a warm, clear night with a million stars. Jeff struggled to look through the viewfinder, trying to position the scope on the moon. He said he could see it, but I knew from his tone he was only humoring his dear old dad. I tried to aim the telescope at Mars, and line everything up for Jeff to see. But he couldn't. I told him to just look for any star, but he found none.

Stepping away from the telescope, Jeff looked up at the open sky. "Do you see stars tonight, when you just look up with your eyes?" he asked.

I said the sky was clear and stars were everywhere.

"I don't see any," he replied, as he squinted.

I looked at him, but was speechless. Jeff walked back into the house. I sat down on a chair, and looked up.

Jeff's sky doesn't have any stars? I spoke out loud. "Jeff's sky doesn't have any stars?"

I really felt God watching me at that moment, from somewhere in that sky full of stars. Where was all of this headed?

I sat outside, gazing at stars, and cried. And I wished. And I prayed.

I think my "account" at the dream bank was finally overdrawn.

****

The pediatric ophthalmologist confirmed Jeff's visual acuity was failing to the point that action must be taken. The gradual progression took five years, from about age seven until twelve. The pea-sized optic chiasm glioma tumor was apparently growing and damaging Jeff's optic nerves, preventing visual information from getting into his brain's visual cortex. No more waiting and observing. Jeff could barely see the "big E" on the Snellen eye chart. Treatment needed to be initiated.

This wasn't an "eye" problem—it was a "brain" problem. Nothing that can be fixed with stronger glasses, or laser surgery or lens implants. Jeff's **eyes** were fine. He just could not get visual information collected on his retinas to travel to the back of his brain. The pathway was partially blocked by the optic glioma. How could such a tiny thing be causing so much trouble? And the concern now was that the tumor would eventually completely block the path of the optic nerves to the visual cortex, leaving him totally blind. Chemotherapy was needed.

It was Jeff who decided to give his optic glioma a name. CLOD. (The spelling is correct). Like a clod of dirt. He liked the sound of it. It was much easier to say than optic glioma. And it sounded nerdy, and disrespectful. He did not want his tumor to have a serious medical name. Optic glioma. That sounded too impressive and stately. He wanted to give it a stupid name. Something kind of dull, slow and non-threatening. CLOD. Something funny. (*Can a brain tumor be funny?*) Jeff wanted to make it so. Something he could tease and taunt. He could threaten it with his treatments. We talked about "frying" CLOD with radiation, and listening to his sizzling screams with each treatment. Put on loud headphones and blast him with Led Zeppelin. Jeff personalized CLOD as the "little nemesis" within him, that he talked about until CLOD just became another member of the family (though black sheep, he was).

Making fun of CLOD was a family effort. Jeff and his parents used humor to create an ongoing game to insult CLOD. Neighbors joined in. There were black CLOD helium balloons tied to strings

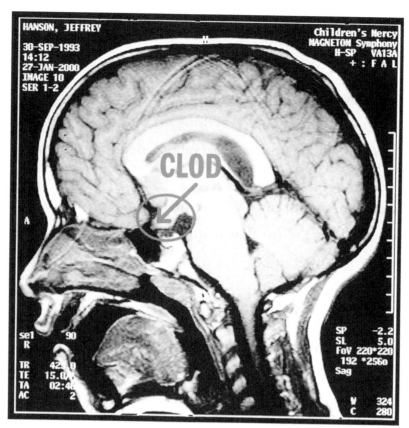

CLOD, as seen on MRI, in Jeff's optic chiasm. Humor was an ongoing tool used to deal with CLOD. We all maintained the attitude that rather than "not talk about it," we did **nothing but** talk about CLOD, which seemed to take away a lot of the fear.

in our back yard, used as targets for BB's or darts. VOTE AGAINST CLOD political signs stood in our yard. There was a "roast CLOD" campaign at Thanksgiving. Anything to degrade CLOD was welcome. The family kept a whole scrapbook dedicated to anti-CLOD activities.

It seems the importance of humor in the face of medical problems, or any adversity for that matter, cannot be overstated. We all yearned for laughter and smiles. Jeff's decision to name his tumor CLOD was a pivotal point in his treatment—a defining moment. It was an attitude adjustment. No matter what happened next, or what the outcome of his vision, CLOD would not be respected or given the satisfaction of eliciting fear or anger. CLOD would only be teased, ridiculed and bullied.

Jeff was faced with a huge medical challenge. **But it was not the challenge, but rather his RESPONSE to the challenge, that was about to define him.**

Your neighbor with rheumatoid arthritis complains all the time about not feeling well. He is in constant pain, and crippled from his ailment. His mobility is limited and his quality of life is terrible. And everyone in the neighborhood knows it. They have all seen it, heard it and lived with it. Your neighbor never stops talking about it. A friend stops you at the corner store and asks you how your neighbor is doing, "you know... the guy with the bad arthritis?" He doesn't have a name. His identity is "the guy with the bad arthritis." Arthritis **defines** him. That is who he is, and what he is. And that is what he does. It's his occupation. To have arthritis. His **response** to the "arthritis challenge" was to "just have arthritis." And when he dies, the obituary won't even need to list his name. GUY WITH

BAD ARTHRITIS DIES. Everybody will know who they mean. His tombstone will say, "John Smith. He had arthritis." And everyone will say, "yes, he sure did!"

No matter what happened next, Jeffrey Owen Hanson was not going to be **defined** by CLOD, the optic glioma. They were two separate living things. Jeff was Jeff. Not the kid down the street with the brain tumor. CLOD was CLOD. Not the tumor that took over a kid's identity.

And Jeff's **response** to the "CLOD challenge" was something quite amazing!

****

Pediatric oncology at Children's Mercy Hospital in Kansas City monitored Jeff from age six, tracking CLOD's behavior with quarterly brain MRI's. When CLOD began affecting Jeff's vision at age 12, in the Fall of 2005, a decision was made to begin an intravenous chemotherapy protocol. This was a huge decision, with a lot of risks and ramifications. A port-a-cath was implanted in his chest to administer the IV medications.

Jeff was in sixth grade. The chemo depressed Jeff's immune system and he needed to avoid people as much as possible. He entered his middle school building through a side door, went straight to his classroom, and stayed there all day with his para. He avoided the lunchroom and large groups. At home, visitors were screened for infectious disease. Activities were limited to indoor games and hobbies.

Jeff lost all of his hair. When he started finding clumps of it on his pillow in the mornings, he asked if he could just have it all cut off. So he had his head "buzzed." He stopped eating and lost

15 pounds. There wasn't any vomiting. Just no appetite. He didn't complain, however. He never cried or seemed depressed about this very scary time in his life. CLOD was going to be eradicated.

But the worst part was, his vision continued to deteriorate. 20/400. And that was only in patchy areas in his visual fields. After 12 weeks of weekly IV infusions, the decision was made to stop the chemotherapy, and switch to radiation therapy (Intensity Modulated Radiation Therapy, or IMRT). Now that is amazing technology. Beams of radiation the width of a human hair, delivered in pulses, are meticulously aimed to hit the irregularly shaped tumor while missing the surrounding normal tissue. Painless, and leaving no outward signs of injury. It was our last hope at preserving any remaining vision.

Meanwhile, at school, it was becoming impossible to continue his studies. Jeff couldn't see anything. All worksheets were magnified. None of his textbooks had large font. He sat in the front row, next to his one-on-one para. Everything was read to him, including exams. There was no point in even being there. A conference was arranged with the school, and they conceded they had nothing to offer Jeff in a mainstream school. And no one knew Jeff's visual future. Was his limited vision going to totally fail? A sober decision was made to transfer Jeff to the Kansas State School for the Blind, to begin Braille before he was totally blind.

The School for the Blind. I had to think about that for a while. Those are words you just don't think you will ever hear. I couldn't even make myself say it. But Jeff truly thought little of it. He was struggling so much academically in his public school, sixth grade, that he actually welcomed a change. He seemed excited that they

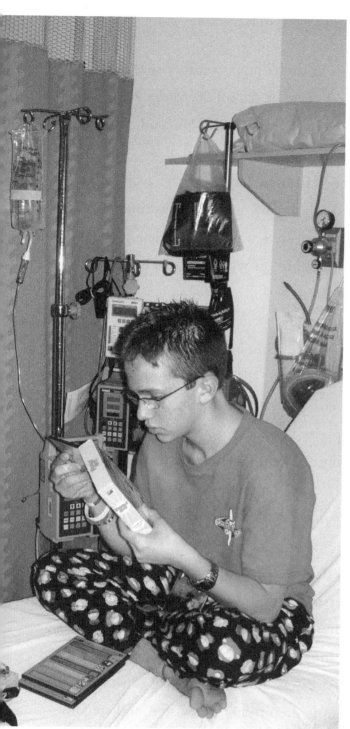

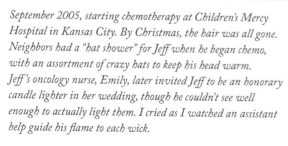

September 2005, starting chemotherapy at Children's Mercy Hospital in Kansas City. By Christmas, the hair was all gone. Neighbors had a "hat shower" for Jeff when he began chemo, with an assortment of crazy hats to keep his head warm. Jeff's oncology nurse, Emily, later invited Jeff to be an honorary candle lighter in her wedding, though he couldn't see well enough to actually light them. I cried as I watched an assistant help guide his flame to each wick.

"accepted" him, even though he didn't know another soul there.

People would ask, "Hey, Jeff, what school do you go to?"

"The Kansas State School for the Blind." He said it proudly, as I kept silent.

I was numb from dreams exiting by now. It didn't even hurt anymore. So much had been taken away by now that I just didn't expect anything in Jeff's future. In a way, I was relieved that Jeff would receive more services and education for what was looking more and more like a world without vision.

I didn't have any more dreams.

Jeff said good-bye to his public school friends, and transferred to the Kansas State School for the Blind (KSSB). *Good-bye to anything that was mainstream for a sixth-grader.* Simply not staying on grade-level in math was looking pretty good about now.

The classroom bell rings. Silently, students find their way out into the hallway. White canes tapping. No running. No shouting. No laughter. *At least Jeff could see well enough to avoid hallway collisions.*

But what seemed pathetic at first, was not as bad as it sounds. KSSB was filled with professionals well-equipped to deal with Jeff's low vision and learning disabilities. Jeff could finally quit trying to be mainstream in anything. He didn't have to keep up with the Jones's any longer. Homework was much easier. The rules were all different. Jeff was very happy, despite his low vision and ongoing treatments to CLOD. The bar was lowered. "Just be the best you can, given what you have to work with." It was a huge relief for his parents, and Jeff adapted amazingly well. There were absolutely no tears or regrets from any of us.

Jeff and CLOD transferred together to KSSB during the sixth-grade semester holiday break. Since Jeff's vision had continued to fail on chemotherapy, he started 28 radiation treatments directed at CLOD, during the month of January, 2006. That was fairly quick and painless for Jeff, but we prayed CLOD did not fare so well. The narrow beam of radiation directed at CLOD for 28 consecutive days was designed to "fry" him, while sparing as much normal surrounding brain tissue as possible. The goal was to preserve Jeff's remaining low vision (20/400 in certain "Swiss cheese" spots in his visual fields). No one suggested his vision might improve after radiation. The damage was already done. And the radiation itself might damage the optic nerves at the target zone, as well. Now it was a "wait and see" situation. There was nothing else to do. No other medical therapy was available for this type of tumor, in this location. It was not operable. Surgery would only damage the chiasm area further. Whether CLOD was really dead or not was uncertain. *Sit back and wait.*

After radiation was completed, the edema in and around CLOD transiently caused even worsening visual acuity. Jeff was on a steroid, dexamethasone, which gave him a dramatic dermatitis on his face. Between that and his patchy, chemo and radiation-stunted hair on the front of his scalp, he was a sight! But I don't think he noticed. I thought it was a "silver lining" that he couldn't see much when he looked in a mirror.

At that time, it seemed every day was a doctor's appointment. Oncology, Genetics, Ophthalmology and Radiation Therapy. Then came Endocrinology to track Jeff's pituitary function, since CLOD had used Jeff's pituitary gland as a recliner chair for the past several years. The pituitary gland was in the radiation target path, and had to be monitored with blood tests to determine if it was damaged. Serial MRI's of the brain were performed, to check for any sign of life in CLOD. Which meant Jeff's orthodontic braces that had recently been put on (they had metal in them), had to be removed for MRI's, and then put on again. While most parents were sitting at basketball games, cheering on their sixth-grader, I sat in waiting rooms praying that CLOD was defeated. I read and reread every issue of *People* and *Good Housekeeping* magazine for the past five years.

****

It was my wife, Julie, Jeffrey's mother, who decided we should have a celebration at the end of radiation therapy, whether it really killed CLOD or not. A big "Farewell to CLOD Extravaganza." Say good-bye with a bang! I was still lost in the emotions of the medical treatments and doing my own personal damage control. I sort of cringed, but went along with it. I thought having a party was a bit strange, but we had talked and teased about CLOD so much that it only seemed appropriate we give him a proper wake. We were all emotionally exhausted by that point, and needed to look forward to something positive and fun. Jeff's blood counts were back to normal and it was fine for him to be around people again. We felt sorry for Jeff, having just changed schools and enduring all the treatments. He didn't seem to feel sorry for himself, however.

Secretly, Julie and friends organized a neighborhood "farewell to CLOD" helium balloon launch in front of our house, when Jeff arrived home from his last radiation treatment. Jeff had already wanted to do something funny on the last day, to surprise the nurses at the radiation center. He had decided he would wear a TUXEDO to his last session! (Remember, he's 12 years old). We laughed at first, but the more we thought about it, "why not?" And this was perfect. He would come back home from radiation, get out of the car wearing a tuxedo, and the yard would be filled with friends and neighbors. Anything to buy a smile.

Jeff definitely turned heads, sitting in that waiting room before his last treatment. We took pictures of him on the treatment table, wearing his radiation target mask in a tuxedo. It was a very funny moment, and **defined** Jeff forever at the radiation center as "the kid in the tuxedo," not the kid with the optic glioma.

Back home, the masses were assembling. February 7, 2006. One hundred friends and neighbors were present, each with a helium balloon in hand. Julie filled the yard with neon posters bidding farewell to CLOD, and celebrating the completion of radiation therapy. Jeff was very surprised, and enjoyed the moment. We handed him a black top hat to cover his scruffy, radiated head, as well as a balloon. A limousine was parked on the street, waiting to take us to Jeff's favorite restaurant.

I stood on our front steps, with a video camera in one hand and my balloon in the other. I gazed into the crowd for a moment, and saw so many supportive faces. We were very blessed. An ophthalmologist. A school teacher. Jeff's former classmates. A man named Bob who stood with his own chemo-balded head, with tears of hope, finding inspiration in Jeff. Friends and neighbors. People that bothered to come to our home, just for ten minutes, to witness a kid's **response** to a challenge. And to bid farewell to Jeff's "little nemesis," CLOD.

I spoke a few words of thanks in a broken voice, and then started

February 7, 2006. Last of 28 radiation treatments. Still haunting to this day, the eerie combination of radiation mask and tuxedo helped us all through a depressing period. Jeff's humor and defiance of CLOD were an inspiration.

Enjoy Each Day!

Thank you Friends

GOOD-BYE CLOD! Julie, Jeff and Hal, on our way to Jeff's favorite restaurant, Macaroni Grill,
immediately after the balloon launch. You can't focus on the home video I shot that day.
My hand was trembling so much that the video gives you vertigo. Curiously, I recently
reviewed the tape to see what color balloon Jeff chose. It was purple, always his favorite.

a countdown from ten. Everyone joined in the counting, until we all shouted "GOOD-BYE CLOD!" Goose bumps, tears and smiles. All 100 balloons sailed into the air. No one quite knew whether to laugh, cheer or cry. Many did all three. It was just one of those exhausting, mixed-emotion experiences.

Despite all the noise, I couldn't hear anything for a moment. Deaf. I was watching all this from a distance. Dead silence. Slow motion. I stared at all the faces wearing a variety of emotions. Through tears, I looked at Jeff and Julie. Time just stood still for a moment. Blank expression on my face, my mind so far away from there. Thinking of where we had just been. For the last five years. The doctors. The treatments. The tears. All the dreams that had slowly slipped away. Our only child. My **dream bank** now empty. How did we ever get to this point? I hoped this was the end of it. Good-bye CLOD. CLOD is dead. I hope. We will never speak of CLOD again.

It didn't seem fair. But why did I ever assume it would be? You shouldn't have to start life out this way. Not when you are 12. You shouldn't even know about MRI's and radiation therapy, port-a-caths and white cell counts. Neurofibromatosis and optic gliomas.

We all gazed upwards at the cloud of multicolored balloons drifting away. Good-bye CLOD. I looked at Jeff in the crowd. He was staring up too, but I was not sure he saw anything once the balloon left his hand. Certainly no stars.

We all face challenges. It is not the challenge, but rather your response to the challenge that defines you.

I looked at Jeff—but was seeing something else now. A premonition, maybe.

In my personal silence, I envisioned a fragile, beautifully colored vase, falling and crashing to the floor—breaking into a hundred pieces. Now it was our job to pick them up and try to put them back together.

Jeff's Bistro

Spring arrived, and with it came warmer days and brighter spirits. We were all in need of a little mental spring cleaning. Jeff's vision stabilized at around 20/150-200 (in scattered spots), after the post-radiation swelling subsided. With that acuity in patchy areas of his visual fields, Jeff learned to accommodate himself to his low vision world. He could watch TV on a large screen if he moved a chair directly in front of the set. He could play computer games on a big screen TV. He could read, slowly, very large fonts (thank you, Microsoft). And he could paint—watercolors on note cards—a hobby that began during chemotherapy, to pass the time. There was actually some normalcy in our family. We got outside. Planted flowers. Talked to the neighbors. Went out to dinner. We played again. We laughed.

Jeff was medically stable. He required no medications for CLOD, after radiation was completed. He was healthy, and felt fine. There was no concern that the optic glioma would metastasize. It wasn't that type of tumor, but other tumors could appear elsewhere in the nervous system at any time. That's just part of neurofibromatosis. Surveillance.

Meanwhile, inside our home, an all out effort to "get rid of stuff we don't use" had begun. It was an annual ritual, but this spring we were doing it big! We planned the garage sale of all garage sales. Jeff thought this really sounded fun, and hoped to make some spending money (enter the entrepreneur). He enjoyed going through all kinds of old toys, videos, computer games, books (many of the things he just couldn't see well enough to enjoy anymore) and clothes to add to the sale. But, also, like any budding entrepreneur, he coerced mom into baking brownies, and he set up a card table featuring beverages and snacks to sell while customers were shopping. He had his own little store. And a captive audience. I assumed he figured he could milk a few extra bucks out of the situation for being "the poor, low vision, chemotherapy kid." But he never played that card.

The garage sale was a big success. It is amazing what people will buy (*remember this later*). Jeff pocketed around $200 and had the most fun in a long time, just socializing with customers and selling his snacks. In fact, he had so much fun that he wanted to do it again—the following week!

Jeff had a goal. We had just remodeled his traditional bedroom into a very contemporary, loft-style, suite. Every design decision was his. It was a reward for being such a trooper through all of his treatments. But the room was lacking one thing—a chair. Not just any chair. Jeff had his eye on a very straight-lined, black, soft leather, Italian Natuzzi recliner he spotted at a neighborhood contemporary furniture store. $1319. Way too expensive for him or his parents.

We wanted to reward him and felt sorry for him—but not that sorry! He was going to have to earn it.

But Jeff had a plan.

Since December, 2005, during chemotherapy, Jeff had a hobby of painting watercolor note cards. It was a pastime to do with visitors, or on his own. It was nothing at first. Just a kid, sitting and painting. Like every kid does. But he loved it. I thought nothing more of it than when he used crayons or "dot art" in his coloring books as a younger child. Something to hang on the refrigerator with a magnet.

This was not a blossoming artist at work. I thought it was kind of pathetic, really. He was twelve—old enough that he should be moving on to more sophisticated activities. Go-karts or model rockets. But because of his low vision and lack of coordination, there were many things around the house Jeff just couldn't do anymore—ping pong, foosball, darts. Even board games were difficult unless he got his face right down to them.

And Reading. Reading became so painful. You just assume your child will eventually pick up a book and read. I always expected Jeff would become an avid reader. We nurtured reading from the day he was born. We went to the local public library every week from age one to eight, picking out books to read at home. We read to Jeff every day. And again at night in bed. But as his vision faded, he never became comfortable as a fluent reader. And about the time I expected him to get lost in the adventures of the Hardy Boys, I found myself still reading about Frank and Joe right there with him. He wouldn't do it on his own. Jeff read too slowly to focus on the story line, when every written word was a concentrated effort.

And homework. Jeff's teachers never realized how difficult it was for him. Julie and I divided up reviewing Jeff's homework assignments, to make certain he got through them. It was a contest to see who got better grades, Julie or I. We did homework together with Jeff every week night, all the way from memorizing vocabulary words to solving the "fifth root of x."

But painting he could do. Friends would come over during chemotherapy and radiation, and they would sit and paint. Julie promoted it. She provided blank note cards, and all the supplies. Kids (and adults) would come and visit, sit with Jeff, and he would invite them to paint a card while they chatted. And when the guests left, Julie would review the day's masterpieces.

What she found was somewhat surprising. Jeff's note cards were bold, fun, colorful and imaginative. And, of course, very abstract. His low vision did not permit him to create any concrete objects. The guests' note cards were drawings of houses with windows, a door, flowers, green grass, blue sky, and a round yellow sun. Jeff's were blocks of bright color, contrasted against unusual and almost shocking, never previously combined colors that just made you stare and smile. Proud, biased, desperate parents? Just grasping for any tiny glimmer of hope? Anything positive? Maybe.

Julie used the note cards for her personal stationery. She encouraged Jeff to continue painting them for her. She tucked them away in a box and saved them for thank-you's and letters. (The guests' note cards went to the trash—sorry family and friends). Together, Jeff and Julie shopped for better card stock paper and supplies. Jeff switched from water colors to acrylics, for brighter, glossy colors and metallics. And the cards kept rolling out. Jeff was a painting machine. He was very creative, and experimented with all sorts

But painting he could do. Wundy the bear, our family mascot, looks over Jeff's shoulder as the watercolor note cards begin to emerge. Grandparents Beverly and Darold Swanson join in the painting (not sure where their cards went) as well as dear friend Vicki, who spent countless hours entertaining and supporting Jeff and our family. Even on vacation in a Florida condo, the cards and paints came along for an activity.

of styles and colors. Julie's friends saw the cards, and asked Jeff to paint some for them, too. Jeff started bundling the cards in six-packs, and selling them to friends and neighbors. At that point, I saw this as nothing more than a sweet gesture on the part of those who knew Jeff's story. Money raised from the sale of the cards was sent to the Children's Tumor Foundation, the organization that raises funds for neurofibromatosis and optic tumor research. Jeff was hoping this might help his own vision, as well as others affected by optic tumors.

With the success of the garage sale, Jeff decided it might be fun and profitable to repeat a morning driveway bake sale, this time featuring his packets of note cards as well. They were colorful and unique, and he would produce them for profit as well as for charity. He was a kid on a mission—to purchase the Italian leather chair. Jeff started painting at a more frantic pace. And he convinced his mother to bake. And bake. Breakfast breads, brownies, marshmallow treats, muffins—you name it. Our poor, single-oven stove never cooled down. Beverages were purchased for resale. Coffee, sodas and water bottles. Jeff needed merchandise, and lots of it! We helped him lay out blank note cards all over our kitchen counters. Jeff would design a card and then paint multiple similar cards, sometimes 100 at a time, but each one an original. We helped him paint the copies. Labels were made for the back of each card, identifying "the artist." Cards were bundled in packages of six and readied for sale. Jeff decided that some of the proceeds from the note cards would continue to go to the Children's Tumor Foundation.

The bake sale needed a name. It couldn't just say "Bake Sale." Jeff needed to "take it up a notch." Hook people. Give it some prestige. He sold coffee, breakfast breads and artwork. What would you name a kiosk like that? "JEFF'S BISTRO." That was it! It sounded sophisticated. It was tongue-in-cheek. He was 12 years old. It was perfect!

Jeff needed advertising. Multicolored, fluorescent, neon posters were created by his mom, and strategically positioned at major intersections near our home. *Jeff's Bistro* was about to become a household name.

A brightly colored, patio umbrella was purchased, to draw attention. Card tables were set up. Caribbean music was playing from a boom box under the table. It was a Monday morning. The Kansas City weather was perfect.

Jeff decided to continue painting, while sitting outside at the *Bistro*. A wise business decision. That was the ultimate grabber. The artist at work. The poor 12-year-old, sitting outside by himself, painting note cards and selling them. I don't think he knew how pathetic this looked, but it worked. Boy did it work!

May 30, 2006. The Bistro umbrella went up promptly at 7:00 a.m. Curious cars slowed to see the kid painting, and waving under the rainbow canopy. A few pulled over for breakfast. Neon signs guided customers to "Garden Dining in Rear," which meant they were invited to sit on our patio and enjoy themselves while they had coffee. The "live" painting and packages of note cards for sale were drawing lots of attention. Neighbors walked over for coffee and pastry. People on their way to work pulled over. Joggers stopped for a water bottle before continuing their exercise. Money exchanged hands.

Opening day of *Jeff's Bistro* was a big success. The umbrella closed at 10:00 a.m. Bottom line… $77. In three hours. That fine leather chair was getting a little closer. Julie and Jeff took the money to the furniture store, and convinced the manager to put the chair

Jeff's Bistro. *Jeff counting the day's "take." The leather chair was in sight. Jeff and Julie cranked out hundreds of loaves of breakfast breads from our small kitchen, while Hal worked in the ER. Neighbors Debbie and Rob take an exercise break at the Bistro.*

Homemade breads, cookies, coffee, hot tea & iced beverages .. breads sold by the slice or whole loaf

VISIONS® - Jeff's custom painted watercolor notecards

"JEFF'S BISTRO"

Smoke-free

Hours vary - if the signs are out, the Bistro is open or call for hours

Garden dining available

Jeff Hanson
CEO President

"on layaway," (something the store had never done before). The manager promised not to sell the chair if Jeff could pay for it in 60 days. Home to paint more note cards and bake more brownies.

The following morning business picked up. Word of mouth and "good reviews," I guess. A few customers were already waiting for their morning coffee when the umbrella went up. Jeff chatted with customers and showed them his note cards. He explained what he was raising money for, and even showed pictures of the Natuzzi leather chair in the local store advertisement. Final tally…$271. Now that was astounding!

Day #3…$103 and everything sold out. Jeff and Julie worked all afternoon and evening to build stock for the next morning. Jeff painted for hours, loving every minute of it. We all joined in, making it a family activity to copy his designs in an assembly line.

Day #4…$240. Incredible! Jeff was ecstatic. He was rapidly achieving his financial goal. I really couldn't believe it. Lemonade stands usually make about $15. I never dreamed his *Bistro* idea would be so successful. I still thought most of this was "pity money" for an unfortunate blind kid. And I assumed the novelty would soon wear off, with both Jeff and the neighborhood. Give him credit for sticking to his strategic plan, and having the work ethic to make it happen.

But that was not the amazing part. Jeff's little business venture apparently affected someone who attended much more than we realized. It seems *Jeff's Bistro* was being thoughtfully watched—from a distance. Unbeknownst to us, Jeff had a secret admirer, and benefactor, who had visited the *Bistro* earlier that morning, and was quite touched by the whole scene. Someone who became totally enthralled with the idea that a 12-year-old kid, in 2006, would sit at the bottom of his driveway, paint note cards, sell baked goods and raise money for a chair for his room. A kid with low vision, who had just endured medical treatments and a battle with CLOD, who now was bound to find **"something I CAN do, instead of whining about what I CAN'T do."** A benefactor with a tender heart, who felt the need to reward energy, enthusiasm, creativity and the entrepreneurial spirit.

And later, on *Bistro* day #4, he decided to pay Jeff a visit.

The *Bistro* was closed for the day, when the door bell rang. An unmarked, white pick-up truck was backing up our driveway. A middle-aged gentleman named Mike, recognized only as a *Bistro* customer from earlier that morning, stood on our front steps. Mike lived just down the street and had seen the *Bistro* unfolding all week. He first met Jeff only earlier that day. I thought our Amish breakfast bread must have made him sick and he was coming to complain.

"I need to speak with Jeff," he smiled. Jeff hesitantly joined me at the front door and we stepped outside with Mike to watch the approaching truck. Two men appeared, and lowered a large cello-wrapped item onto our driveway. Mike smiled widely. Jeff slowly approached the delivery, until his low vision permitted him to see what was now sitting in our driveway. The Natuzzi leather chair. Jeff looked up at Mike. "But how did you know? I've only paid for part of it. I can't get it yet."

"I went to that store you showed me in the ad today, and paid for all of it," Mike explained. He then proceeded to give Jeff back the money that Jeff had already paid down. I was dumbfounded. You talk about your random acts of kindness! Holy Cow! That was $1300 bucks! Julie cried. Jeff hugged Mike. Mike hugged Jeff. Julie hugged Mike and Jeff. I joined in the hugging.

"But why did you do this?" Jeff asked, as he unwrapped the recliner and plopped down in it.

"Because I wanted to. This was easy for me. Much easier than what you are doing. I wanted to do something for you, to applaud you for your ambition and great spirit! I just don't know any kids who are doing this. They are all playing soccer, or video games. Doing what everyone else does. I just wanted you to realize how unique you are. You are not handicapped or impaired at all. You are a winner! And here is your trophy to prove it."

Jeff pushed back the chair to the full recline position. "You gotta try this, Mike. This chair is even better than I thought." They traded places, and Mike leaned back. It was a comical sight, at noon, in the middle of our driveway. We waved at cars going past.

"The reason I am not doing what everyone else does, is because I can't."

"Yes, but I sure don't see you having a pity party about it." Mike sat up.

"No, I'm not that way. I'm really having a blast. My *Bistro* is a lot of fun, to make things and see how much I can sell. But wait—now that I have the chair, my goal doesn't mean anything anymore. The *Bistro* was just getting started. I don't want to stop now. I wanted to do this all summer." Jeff looked at Julie and I.

"Just because I bought you the chair, doesn't mean I want you to stop your *Bistro*. In fact, I want you to keep doing the *Bistro*. You just got your payment early, that's all."

"So do you want me to pay you back at the end of the summer?"

"No. I want you to pay it forward to someone else. Someone who needs the money a lot more than me or you. Think about it.

The Natuzzi chair lands on our driveway. Mike and family, with Jeff and Julie. The chair immediately found its new home in Jeff's remodeled room. Things like this just don't happen (do they?).

Pick who you want. The money I refunded you today—give that away, too."

Generosity begets generosity.

Mike went on to tell Jeff that he, too, was visually impaired. And he was touched that some of the note card sales benefitted a charity devoted to researching eye tumors in children.

Generosity begets generosity.

Jeff then told Mike that he would continue *Jeff's Bistro* for the summer and that all future *Bistro* profits would benefit the Children's Tumor Foundation. He had his reward, his trophy—the leather chair. He didn't need anything else. It was settled. They shook hands. The chair was carried up our stairway and positioned in Jeff's newly remodeled room. Perfect!

Mike and Jeff hugged again, and Mike left. They never spoke of this again. The three of us stood and stared at the black recliner. It had fallen out of the sky and landed on our driveway. What just happened? Four days into the *Bistro*, and there was the chair. **Why** did that happen? *(Thank you, Mike, for that incredible act of kindness and generosity)*.

I think Jeff slept in the chair that night.

****

From that point on, *Jeff's Bistro* took on a new focus. It was a fundraiser. Not for Jeff or his parents, but for charity. For the Children's Tumor Foundation. We all felt challenged to see just how much money we could raise in one summer. It became a family obsession. And it was an incredible amount of work and fun!

This period of time gave opportunity for all three of us to examine our personal goals, and evaluate what was really important

41

to us. Moving forward in the "post-CLOD" era, we needed to clarify our values and purpose. How were we now **defined** by others and by ourselves? *Hopefully not the house where CLOD lived!* Did people define us differently than how we **wished** to be defined? All three of us now realized we had the power to control this. And our mutual response was that our family wanted to be **defined by generosity.**

Long before Julie and I had Jeffrey in our lives, Julie often described her "rules of successful parenting." She was a firm believer in church and Sunday School, teaching moral and ethical values and instilling independence in your children. She vowed to raise a child with purpose and a loving, giving heart. And prayed for a child who found their passion and pursued it—outside our home, on their own—none of this "failure to launch" stuff. Three criteria. Happy, independent and giving back to the world. The latter was coming to fruition.

Jeffrey Owen Hanson, President and CEO of *Jeff's Bistro*, made some executive decisions. The *Bistro* would be held every Saturday morning through the summer, from 7:00 a.m. until "sell-out." That would give us a whole week to build inventory of baked goods and note cards between bistros. All future proceeds would go to the Children's Tumor Foundation (CTF). We would also solicit cash donations, and disseminate information to increase awareness about neurofibromatosis and optic gliomas.

Sales at *Jeff's Bistro* skyrocketed! When people found out where the funds were going, they became even more generous. Many inspired people became regular customers. People would stand in line before the umbrella went up, to get a whole loaf of the lemon poppy seed bread or the cherry cream cheese breakfast bread. Blueberry cinnamon cream cheese streusel or coconut pecan cream cheese banana bread. (Yes, Julie likes to bake).

The week's creation of newly hand-painted note cards flew off the table. Friends and families would meet for breakfast on our patio. And people didn't just pay regular price for their goodies. They started tipping. And donating cash. And writing checks to the CTF. Cars would slow down and just hand money out the window. The *Bistro* was a "cash cow!" Jeff was in heaven.

The Saturday tallies kept climbing. $409...$429...$784...$1625!!! *The Kansas City Star* appeared with a photographer to learn about the low vision kid raising money for optic tumor research. The *Bistro's* multicolored umbrella was splashed across the front page. TV interviews. Curiosity seekers from all over the city came to meet 12-year-old Jeff, have a muffin, and leave a donation. It was phenomenal. Jeff just figured this was how lemonade stands were. CLOD was long forgotten.

August 5, 2006. An extraordinary day. Beautiful weather, and the biggest turnout yet. There were probably $3000 in cash and checks lying on the card table. Cars were parked up and down the street. I was chatting with a neighbor when I noticed an unmarked Overland Park police car pull up. Two plain clothes officers got out and seemed to be surveying our operation. They pretended to be shopping. Thoughts were racing through my head of which particular city codes we were violating. No, we did not have a permit for a business, a public meeting or to be a city vendor. No, we did not notify the city of an event that might cause traffic congestion. No, we weren't a 501(c)3. But, we weren't planning to bilk the public with fraudulent charity fundraising and then take the money. No, we weren't going to pay sales tax to the city or State of Kansas.

An officer approached me. *OK...what does he want?* My heart was pounding.

"I got the best poppy seed muffin here last Saturday. Do you have any of those this week?"

I smiled. "Why yes, we do, officer. In fact, today, they are free!"

Ah...another satisfied customer. He left Jeff a $5 tip.

And then, to top off the day, we were just about to close when a late arriving customer, Dennis, appeared. It was his first visit to the *Bistro*, he had driven 45 minutes, and he was disappointed to see that we were virtually sold out of everything. He took the single remaining marshmallow treat, which wasn't even looking that good in the August sun. Dennis introduced himself to Jeff, and then proceeded to hand him a check...for $1000! He explained that he budgeted a certain amount of money each year for charity, and this year he decided to benefit Jeff's cause, the Children's Tumor Foundation.

Generosity begets generosity.

At summer's end, *Jeff's Bistro* gifted the Children's Tumor Foundation with $15,000. What an incredible, unpredictable summer. So much work, but so much fun! Only six months after completing radiation therapy. We never dreamed joy could come back to us so quickly.

School was starting up again at the Kansas State School for the Blind—seventh grade. Jeff's low vision remained stable. We needed to get back into our routine.

Jeff continued to paint note cards for another year. All told, Jeff hand-painted approximately 5000 original cards for charity.

As I packed away the multicolored umbrella, I stood in our garage and looked out at our empty driveway. I sighed. And I smiled. From somewhere inside me, after five years of hidden tears, came a genuine, spontaneous smile.

Jeff's Bistro. How could such a silly little idea turn into such a big thing? I saw Mike in the leather recliner chair, and Jeff under the umbrella, painting. Crowds of generous people. Our summer of charitable giving. Jeff was very happy. We all were. Generosity was a lot of fun. Jeff was defined by generosity.

The shattered vase maybe wasn't quite as bad as I thought. The broken pieces still found purpose. It would never be as a father dreamed, but…the colors were still there, and a new form was taking shape.

I closed the garage door.

We thought that was the end of the story.

THE BEGINNING ...

Screaming, playful colors adorned the *Bistro* note cards. Originally painted with limited watercolors, the 5" x 7" cards gradually transitioned from pale pastels to brilliant acrylics and metallics. The first primitive, low vision cards evolved into more complex, sophisticated free-style patterns. Jeff is shown with an early acrylic on canvas, later gifted to Kansas City's Children's Mercy Hospital Oncology Clinic.

Evening with Elton

The Make-A-Wish Foundation has been granting fantastic, almost impossible to imagine wishes to children with life-threatening medical conditions since 1980. Their website boasts over 230,000 wishes granted, currently at the rate of a wish every 38 minutes. The average "wish" costs the organization around $8000. A compassionate team of staff, volunteers and donors coordinates the "wish-granting" of downtrodden kids and their families, who are in dire need of something fun and positive in their stressed-out lives. A one week getaway from their medical condition and treatments. Close your eyes to the problems of the medical world, deny your illness, and just go have uninterrupted fun.

And the fun isn't just **any** fun. It is **special** fun! Fun you just couldn't arrange on your own. Fun that involves bending the rules, cutting to the front of the line, getting to go places kids don't usually get to go. Behind the scenes. In the Green Room. In the Locker Room. In the cockpit. In the Oval Office—kind-of-fun. Meeting people that nobody gets to meet. Staying in places you never dreamed you would go.

I had always (wrongfully) assumed that "wish kids" were suffering from terminal illnesses and were financially destitute. Not so. Many wish kids eventually recover from their serious medical conditions and go on to lead normal, healthy lives. And the trauma of serious medical illness crosses all socioeconomic boundaries. Any progressive, degenerative or malignant medical condition might qualify a child for a "wish," and financial need is not a criterion for selection. The child's physicians and medical team recommend them to Make-A-Wish, who then contacts the family to determine what wish is desired. The child and family often consider several possible wishes before they make their final decision.

Make-A-Wish approached Jeff in January of 2006, during radiation therapy. He was going blind from an optic nerve tumor. I was, at first, threatened by the whole idea. I didn't want to meet with them. Jeff wasn't dying. And we weren't destitute. *Give the wish to some other kid. Somebody who was sick—terminal.* Having Make-A-Wish show up on your front step seemed like the final surrender to CLOD and our life-long battle. The grim reaper. One last cigarette. Thanks, but no thanks! (*But it wasn't about me*).

Jeff was excited about the idea. He immediately saw it as an opportunity for a fun break from trips to the doctor, radiation center, IV's and brain MRI's. He was thrilled! And we soon learned what the Make-A-Wish Foundation was really about.

But what was his wish? That's not so easy. Think about it. You're a kid. You can have just about anything you want—within reason. A PlayStation. A laptop. Sit on the bench with the Patriots or the

Packers. Do something daring. Meet a celebrity. Your idol. Travel. Disney World!!! It's endless.

Jeff considered several options over a few months. He definitely wanted to meet someone famous rather than travel somewhere. He could travel anytime. **That** we could arrange on our own. But meeting a celebrity—you need some help to accomplish that. You can't just book an appointment with Miley Cyrus or Celine Dion.

But Jeff had criteria for his "wish celebrity." They couldn't just be a current star. They needed to have longevity. Someone who had been around for awhile. No "one hit wonder" of today. He didn't want to meet this person, and then in a couple of years have no one remember who they were. Some previous star from a TV show that was now off the air. What fun would that be to brag about? No, they needed to be a superstar, not just with his generation, but proven over the years. Worthy of bragging rights for the rest of his life. Sports legends, though frequently requested as wishes, were definitely off Jeff's list. Jeff was not into sports at all, given his low vision. But someone he loved, a movie star, or musician, or artist or politician who had stood the test of time. But on the level of an Elvis, a Michael Jackson, an Elizabeth Taylor, a Kennedy.

And they needed to have a heart. Famous, not infamous. A celebrity with a reputation for being compassionate, respected for their good deeds and constantly newsworthy for their profession and their philanthropy.

Well, that narrows it right down now, doesn't it?

Sir Elton John is one of the most prolific, popular music singer/songwriters of all time. Throughout his 45+ year musical career, he has written and recorded more than 30 albums, including seven consecutive No. 1 albums with more than 50 top 40 hits and nine No. 1 singles. He has won six Grammy Awards, an Academy Award for *The Lion King* (best original song, "Can You Feel the Love Tonight," with lyricist Tim Rice, 1994) and a Tony Award for *Aida*, (best original score, with lyricist Tim Rice, 2000). On September 6, 1997, Elton performed a reworked version of "Candle in the Wind, 1997" at the funeral of Diana, Princess of Wales, in Westminster Abbey. That tribute went on to become the biggest-selling single of all time, eventually selling over 33 million copies worldwide. Proceeds benefitted Diana's memorial fund. In 2008, *Billboard* magazine named Elton John as the most successful male solo artist on "The Billboard Hot 100 Top All-Time Artists"—and third overall, most successful act, behind only The Beatles and Madonna. (Did I mention he also plays the piano?)

With regard to philanthropy, Elton founded the Elton John AIDS Foundation (EJAF) in 1992, raising public awareness about the condition. The Foundation, a "FOUR STAR" charity as voted by Charity Navigator, works to eliminate prejudice and discrimination against affected individuals, such as the highly publicized Ryan White story—the hemophiliac teenager infected by blood transfusion. EJAF has raised over $300 million dollars, funding AIDS prevention programs, research and treatments for those who can't afford medications. In 1995, Elton was made a Commander of the Order of the British Empire (CBE). He was knighted by Queen Elizabeth II for his charitable work, in 1998. **Sir** Elton John.

Why all this discussion about Elton John? You guessed it. That's who Jeff wanted to meet for his Make-A-Wish! Sir Elton John. Longevity? Uh-huh. Superstar? Yep. Still current? Just pick up any

People magazine. Philanthropist? Are you kidding me? $300 million to charity! Bragging rights? Proudly! He's the piano playing, singing, song writing, Electric Boots, Mohair Suit, Saturday Night Fighting, Musical Genius, Rocket Man of all time!!! Jeff listened to Elton's hits since he was two years old. He would often spin dad's old vinyl copies of "Crocodile Rock" and "Bennie and the Jets." "Tiny Dancer" and "Levon." Being born in 1993, Jeff grew up with *The Lion King* and its Academy Award winning soundtrack. Jeff had even seen (from rafter seats) Elton in concert with mom and dad, when he was six, and stood on his chair and danced the night away—in awe that this was the same voice from the vinyl records, in person!

But meeting Elton John? Now this would take some doing. And time. And scrambling on the part of Make-A-Wish. For starters, Sir Elton is a hard star to catch. He is constantly touring the globe, with many irons in the fire. He's harder to get a "sit down" with than the Pope. He has been "paparazzied" to death over the years, and has a lot of filters between himself and a 12-year-old fan—rightfully earned filters. And he had never granted a Make-A-Wish. Not because he didn't want to, but because when Elton was a teen idol in the 70's, the Make-A-Wish Foundation did not exist. And current "wish kids" choose current teen stars, or Disney World trips for their wishes. They don't go for longevity and philanthropy. But Jeff had a different strategy.

It took a year and a half to catch up with Elton. In fact, we had all given up and nearly forgotten about "the wish." Jeff's Bistro had come and gone. Seventh grade at the Kansas State School for the Blind had come and gone. Jeff's vision had stabilized at a remarkable 20/80, in patchy areas, which was much better than anyone predicted. He had to get fairly close to someone before he could recognize them, but that was much better than immediately after radiation. Jeff continued to paint note cards for charity, now acrylic, and was transitioning to acrylics on canvas. And he was having some success **selling** canvases, and gifting canvases to charities for auction. Jeff gave proceeds from the sale of his art to the Children's Tumor Foundation and other children's charities. I figured "the wish" had lost its meaning, since Jeff's treatments were completed and he was just being monitored for any recurrence of CLOD. His vision was poor, but very stable, for the moment.

Make-A-Wish had just about given up on the request, also. They had twice come back to Jeff, asking him to choose a different wish. Booking a "sit down" with Elton was at a stalemate. But Jeff stuck to his guns. He was holding out for Elton. So, the time just passed.

It was October, 2007, twenty months after the last radiation treatment and the farewell to CLOD balloon launch, when we received a phone call from our Make-A-Wish "wish granter." Kansas City's brand new downtown events center was announcing its grand opening. "The Sprint Center proudly announces the opening night extravaganza, with a live performance by...ELTON JOHN AND HIS BAND." We had seen it advertised in the newspaper. But tickets—all 18,000 of them—sold out in a few hours. Oh well, we didn't want to fight the crowd anyway. And Jeff couldn't see from the rafters anymore.

But our wish-granter had astounding news. Sir Elton John had agreed to meet with Jeff, now 14, and his parents, before the performance. Back stage. And Make-A-Wish had VIP seats for the three of us. And a limo. And dinner before the show. We were totally surprised, and elated! Jeff was ecstatic.

We talked about this a lot before the big day. We would only have a few minutes with Elton back stage. We wanted to plan our conversation a little, so Jeff covered all the questions he had. What do you say to a world renowned superstar? Why did you choose him as your wish? What could Elton John possibly find interesting in our boring Kansas lives? We joked that Elton was finally going to get **his** wish, to meet Jeffrey Owen Hanson in person!

Jeff wanted to briefly tell Elton his medical story, and why he was a "wish kid" in the first place. But mainly, he wanted to tell Elton about his art and philanthropy. Jeff felt this was their common ground. Deep down, Jeff admired Elton for his philanthropic spirit. Jeff was fully aware of Elton's work for AIDS in Africa, and his support of orphanages there. Jeff felt Elton would be a great mentor for his art, and planned to bring some hand-painted note cards as a gift, to show Elton how he raised money for the Children's Tumor Foundation. What Jeff did not want to do, was **ask** for anything. It was enough just to have a few minutes of his time, for a photograph, an autograph, and conversation. We could only imagine how many people must **want something** from a celebrity.

The day arrived, October 13, 2007. I was nervous. Julie was nervous. Jeff wasn't nervous at all. Our wish-granter met us for dinner, and the limo took all four of us to the Sprint Center. There was a huge crowd, and I didn't see how we would navigate all the security to get through to back stage. But we were eventually met by Elton's staff member, who got us through the hoops to the Green Room. There were several other people there partying, and we assumed they were all waiting to meet Elton, like us, for various reasons. We thought

Elton would enter the room soon and greet everyone. But we quickly learned that no one there expected to even get a back-stage glimpse of the superstar, and they were all doubtful and astounded that we thought we would.

Soon, a staff member invited us to an "even greener," Green Room. The crowd was suddenly left behind. Just Jeff, Julie, myself and Jeff's wish-granter, Debbie. The four of us sat in a dimly lit, quiet, comfortable lounge filled with lavish food and beverages. There were fresh flowers, and scented candles. We sat on over-stuffed leather furniture. Elton's little slice of home on the road. It was so secluded you would never have known there was a huge crowd congregating outside. *This was it!* Jeff was finally going to get his Make-A-Wish.

We all chatted nervously until suddenly, from out of the blue, A DOG RAN INTO THE ROOM, and stopped where Jeff was sitting. *(No, please! Not now! Not at this moment. Things were so perfect)*. A black and white Cocker Spaniel. I immediately thought the pooch somehow managed to get into the building on grand opening night, and was running around trying to find his way out. Poor frightened thing. I started to say something... until I noticed the collar...a very beautiful and elaborate collar...and then realized this was no Kansas City stray. Jeff got down on the floor and started petting the dog.

And then Elton spoke as he entered the room, "Oh, I see you have met Arthur. He travels with me everywhere. And you must be Jeffrey."

Pinch self!

It was him. The man we had seen on TV, in magazines, in concert. The voice we had listened to for 40 years. That British accent.

The costume. The shoes. The jewelry. The GLASSES! Ready to go on stage.

Jeff stood up from Arthur and extended his hand. "Do you like to be called **Sir** Elton, or Elton?" (Fortunately, there was still one person in the "extremely Green Room" who wasn't star struck).

"Please…Elton."

Greetings were exchanged and Jeff and Elton had a wonderful visit. We tried to just stand back and watch. Elton immediately inquired about Jeff's medical status and his vision, knowing this meeting was orchestrated by Make-A-Wish. And we were happy to report Jeff's vision was patchy, but stable around 20/80. Jeff gave Elton some hand-painted "VISIONS" note cards, and told him about *Jeff's Bistro*, his fundraising for charity, and his art. Jeff told Elton he was now painting acrylics on canvas, and donating the paintings to charitable auctions. He was having enough success selling his canvases that he was also able to make cash donations to various children's organizations.

Elton was very compassionate and generous with his time. Jeff asked for an autograph, and came prepared with a large poster board and marker.

"Write big, Elton, remember I can't see very well." Elton complied, and gave him a lifetime keepsake.

Elton encouraged Jeff. They talked about The Elton John AIDS Foundation, Africa, and charitable giving. Elton seemed genuinely interested in Jeff's art, and heart, and philanthropy at such a young age. I suspect this meeting wasn't what he expected.

Elton told Jeff, **"If you give to the world, the world will give back."**

In the circle, the circle of life.

Some say eat or be eaten

Some say live and let live

But all are agreed as they join the stampede

You should never take more than you give!

(From "Circle of Life," *The Lion King*, lyrics by Tim Rice, music by Elton John—1994)

Jeff then reached in his pocket, and pulled out a check...for The Elton John AIDS Foundation...for $1000. "This is for your foundation. It's money I've earned selling note cards and canvases. I like to give the money to charities that help children, like the AIDS orphans in Africa that you support."

There was a pause. Elton looked at the check. I can't speak for Elton John, but I suspect he was astounded. Who ever gives him anything? Back stage. At a "meet and greet/photo-op/autograph signing."

Jeff Hanson, an eighth grader at the Kansas State School for the Blind, Make-A-Wish kid, artist, and PHILANTHROPIST? I can only imagine the thoughts running through Elton's head. *This is the Make-A-Wish kid I was told to meet tonight before the show? Jeff chose to meet me, for 15 minutes, and then gave EJAF a check for $1000? Jeff, you blew it!!! You could have gone to Disney World! Or a cruise! But you chose to meet me, and give me your hard earned money?*

Well, I guess Jeff stuck to his guns. He certainly didn't **ask** Elton for anything. And Jeff was loving this. It was just like *Jeff's Bistro*. Generosity was fun. Jeff was still **defined by generosity**, a year and a half later. It was way more fun to give the money away, knowing how many people it could help.

Elton asked his staff to take a picture of Jeff handing him the check, and I snapped a couple myself. (A blown-up copy of that picture still hangs in Jeff's bedroom).

The $1000 check for EJAF.
It represents a lot of hand-painted
note cards. Jeff told us he wanted to
do this on the day of the concert.
We enlarged a copy of the real check,
so Jeff could read it and show it to
Elton. Jeff stood on his chair for
"I'm Still Standing." Jeff and
Make-A-Wish "wish granter"
Debbie went shopping for EJ
souvenirs after the concert.

Time was running short. We could now hear the rumble of 18,000 cheering fans. Jeff and Elton were talking about all the places Elton had traveled and performed. We had recently taken a Mediterranean cruise that stopped at Kusadasi, Turkey. We had visited the ruins of Ephesus. We knew that Elton had performed there, in the excavated amphitheater, and we actually had a DVD of that performance. Jeff asked how they ever got a grand piano into that place, and they discussed the logistics.

But then the topic switched to Dubai. Jeff asked Elton if he had ever traveled there, and seen the man-made islands shaped like palm trees and the world globe. Jeff had seen all about Dubai on TV, and was fascinated with it. Elton said indeed he had been there, and it was fantastic.

Then things happened quickly. I thought we needed to leave soon, to get to our seats. But then if Elton John was with us, back stage, I guess we weren't missing anything too important. I could hear the audience clapping and stomping their feet, and I glanced at my watch. It was 8:03 pm. I felt a silly, guilty feeling, like we were making 18,000 people wait for us to chit-chat. I was getting nervous that we were making Elton late for his performance, but he didn't seem that stressed about it. Elton turned to his staff member, and inquired when they would be in Dubai again.

"In three months, in January."

Oh, God!

(Get ready!) Elton turned to Jeff and asked, "Jeff, would you be able to get out of school in January, to come to Dubai?"

Stunning silence.

The next three seconds lasted about an hour in my brain. *Let's weigh this out. Let me see now. Missing a few days at the Kansas State School for the Blind, versus flying to Dubai with Elton John. Hmmmmm. I don't know. What exactly is he asking here?*

Jeff turned to me, like he needed permission to speak. Or he was speechless, I'm not sure. I was. Things were getting surreal.

I looked over at Julie. No help there. I finally broke the silence with "I guess you will have to call in sick."

"Good, he'll call in sick then," Elton laughed. He turned to his staff and asked them to make all the travel arrangements. "We'll be in touch with you. We'll fly all three of you there so we can spend more time together."

Elton stood from his chair. "I really must meet with someone else before the show. It was a pleasure to meet you all. Jeff, we will have more time to talk in Dubai."

Everyone hugged.

"Elton, are you going to play my favorite song?"

"What's your favorite song?"

"I'm Still Standing."

Tears were immediately in my eyes, and my heart was breaking.

"Yes, we are going to play your favorite song." They hugged again, and we parted. I wasn't really sure if it was good-bye, or not. It didn't sound like it. Dubai?

Back in our third row, piano-front seats, we settled in for the show. Whew! A lot just happened in the last 15 minutes. All three of us were numb. What did he just say? Did we hear this right? Are we going to Dubai with Elton John? This was such an unbelievable situation, I couldn't quite grasp it.

Generosity begets generosity.

The Kansas City concert was fantastic. We sang and danced the night away. And it was strangely magical that the man we were just talking to was now rocking the house down. What a fabulous grand opening this was for the Sprint Center. And what a fabulous closure to the whole CLOD chapter of Jeff's life. Make-A-Wish came through with a "trip of a lifetime." And Elton...you are totally amazing!

Near the end of the concert, Elton shouted out, "Jeff, this one's for you!" He broke into "I'm Still Standing," which is a real crowd pleaser. Jeff stood on his chair for the entire song, singing and waving his arms. I'm not sure Jeff really saw Elton from the third row. He saw the colored lights of the stage. He saw the piano, and the colored costume moving back and forth across the keyboard. But he **heard** it all!

> *Don't you know I'm still standing better than I ever did*
> *Looking like a true survivor, feeling like a little kid*
> *I'm still standing after all this time*
> *Picking up the pieces of my life without you on my mind...*
> *(CLOD!)*

("I'm Still Standing," music by Elton John, lyrics by Bernie Taupin, from *Too Low for Zero*, 1983)

The concert was on a Saturday night. On Monday afternoon, Jeff received a call from the president of the Children's Tumor Foundation, in New York. They knew of Jeff because of the money he had been sending them since *Jeff's Bistro*.

"Jeff, do you know Sir Elton John? For some reason, he just sent us $5000 in your honor."

Generosity begets generosity.

****

For the next three months, there were many moments when the three of us thought *that never happened! He didn't say that. He's a very busy man. He doesn't have time for us.* But it wasn't just words. Or a dream. Elton really did invite us to Dubai. And as the date approached, Elton's staff notified us with all the details. We were off to Dubai with Elton John and the band!

January 19, 2008, we boarded a jet in Kansas City and flew First Class to JFK, and then on to Dubai. The long trip was well worth the wait.

Our hotel and the location of Elton's concert were in Abu Dhabi, United Arab Emirates, at the *Emirates Palace.* (Check that place out online—a self-proclaimed "Seven Star" hotel). Over-the-top, ten!

After sleeping all night on a plane, we arrived in Dubai at 10:00 p.m. (just in time for bed). We had a reservation for three nights. Jeff had a palatial room next door to mom and dad. Our circadian rhythms were totally messed up, and none of us could sleep. We really weren't sure when Elton would be arriving. The following morning we arranged a tour of the area, went "dune bashing" in the Abu Dhabi desert in an SUV, and visited a camel farm.

When we returned to our rooms in the afternoon, there was a phone message for Jeff. Elton and staff invited us to dinner in Elton's suite! What a thrill! Jeff was so excited. We all were. The concert would not be until the following evening.

The three of us showered (you need to do this after visiting a camel farm), and dressed for dinner. This was a bit of a struggle. What do you wear in Dubai, when Sir Elton John invites you to his suite for dinner? Dress up? Flashy? Dress down? Casual? "Just be yourself," Jeff said. Always the sensible one.

The iconic Burj Al Arab *hotel in Dubai. Every picture of Jeff at the camel farm shows Jeff wincing and frowning because camel farms don't smell very good.*

We met a staff member in the hotel lobby (about the size of a foot-ball field), who escorted us to an exclusive part of the hotel. Very secure. President George Bush had just stayed in Elton's suite the week prior. We were treated like royalty.

Elton greeted Jeff and his parents like we were old friends. I thought a lot about this, later. Elton really went out of his way to make us feel comfortable. We laughed at how *thrilled* Elton's staff must have been, to get to spend their free night in Dubai entertaining perfect strangers—a visually impaired 14-year-old boy and his parents, from Kansas. I'm sure they rolled their eyes when they found that out. But you would have never known it. The hospitality was tremendous. We were treated like we were the most important people in the U.A.E.

We spent several hours together, just talking and eating. Jeff got every question answered, from Elton's childhood challenges, grow-ing up in England, to music, movies, favorite cars, favorite stars, not-so-favorite stars, boats, AIDS, Africa, art and philanthropy. And Elton was curious to learn about Jeff's vision, his medical journey, his art, philanthropy and our family life in Kansas.

Jeff unboxed a large canvas for Elton that was specially painted as a thank you for the trip. (Yes, we dragged it on a plane half way around the world). It was very colorful and abstract, and depicted Jeff's "distorted" view (filtered through CLOD remnants) of Elton performing on stage, under bright lights.

"It's called *View from the 22nd Row.*"

Elton leaned the canvas against the wall, and then sat down and stared at it. Jeff waited for a response. "It's a line from your song, 'Candle in the Wind.'"

"I know it's from my song," Elton laughed. "So this is what you see when you look in the distance?"

"Pretty much."

Jeff explained that his art had now progressed to acrylics on canvas, using ideas adapted from his note cards. Jeff went on to share that his paintings were often donated to charity live auctions, and also sold for profit. Elton encouraged Jeff to continue exploring and developing his art.

The conversation turned to the Elton John AIDS Foundation (EJAF), and the huge effort to help orphans of AIDS in South Africa. Elton described communities he had visited where there were NO ADULTS—they had all died of AIDS. Only children lived in the village. Jeff was very disturbed by this, and wanted to help. Jeff told Elton that his art benefitted many children's organizations, and that he would like to continue donating to EJAF.

Elton looked at Jeff's canvas again, and then asked Jeff if he would be willing to paint for an orphanage that EJAF supports, to decorate their walls. Jeff was thrilled with the idea. At age 14, Jeff was very touched by the plight of children his own age and younger, in such a dreary situation. And it was a means for Jeff to gift and thank Elton, in a small way, for his generosity and compassion.

So the deal was settled. Jeff would paint for Elton, to lift the spirits of the kids living at the Baphumelele orphanage in South Africa. I'm sure Elton intended to reimburse Jeff for his costs of supplies and shipping, but I knew Jeff would accept no money for this. This would be his gift. Jeff was earning enough money from his art sales to fund this project. Jeff would create the art and gift it to EJAF.

We talked and laughed until midnight. We didn't want the evening to end. (I think I caught Elton yawning, probably jet lag).

Jeff presented Elton with View from the 22nd Row. *Jeff's room at the* Emirates Palace *in Abu Dhabi. Posing with EJ in his dressing room in Abu Dhabi. Sorry about the camera causing Elton's "red eye."*

An amazing meeting in a foreign, magical place, for a kid from Kansas. *(Well, Jeff, you did all right on the Make-A-Wish choice. Sorry Disney World).*

Running on adrenaline, there was time for sight-seeing and shopping the following day. And that evening we were invited to Elton's dressing room before the outdoor concert, for a brief farewell visit back stage.

But it wasn't farewell. Elton wanted Jeff to come to Las Vegas to see his show there, The Red Piano, at Caesar's Palace. So we spent a few minutes comparing calendars (Elton's was more filled than ours), and landed on a date in June. Here we go again!

It was Elton who helped the low vision kid down the dark, back-stage stairs in Abu Dhabi. We parted in the dark with a hug. We joined the crowd out front. Elton walked on stage as the crowd roared.

The concert was spectacular! Abu Dhabi wasn't used to this. The outdoor stage and seating were constructed specifically for this show only. The Arab world was rocking to "Saturday Night's All Right for Fighting!" But amazingly, even people in the U.A.E. knew the words to the songs. (International superstar? Longevity? Bragging rights?).

Near the end of the concert, Elton gave a touching dedication to Jeff and our family, and then sang "Circle of Life." We cried. *You should never take more than you give*, seemed to strike home more than ever. Generosity and philanthropy had become very important to all three of us. We really knew what he meant. He knew we knew.

****

June 11, 2008, The Forum at Caesar's Palace, Las Vegas. *The Red Piano* show was sensational! A car whisked us away after the show, to Elton's residence in Vegas. A dinner was waiting for us, with Elton and his staff. We talked and laughed for hours. Jeff brought photographs of the artwork he had created for the EJAF supported orphanage in South Africa. Twelve, brightly colored canvases, with an African theme—several of them depicting abstract African animals, for the children to enjoy. And to generate money from the art, six of the canvases were photographed and printed as "Art for Africa" note cards for sale, with all proceeds going to EJAF.

Amazingly, the wooden crate containing those twelve canvases arrived at the Baphumelele Children's Home in Khayelitsha, South Africa, on Christmas Eve. The children helped unpack them. We made an international phone call there on Christmas morning and spoke to Mama Rosie, who thanked Jeff and confirmed the children were already making crayon drawings, trying to copy the paintings. Jeff was thrilled that the canvases survived the long trip safely, and were now bringing joy to the children.

There have been other meetings with Elton since then, the highlight probably being the 2010 *White Tie and Tiara Ball* at Elton's Woodside Estate in Old Windsor, England. This is a magnificent formal garden party, dinner and auction featuring world class entertainment, hosted by Elton and partner David Furnish, with proceeds benefitting the Elton John AIDS Foundation. The guest list is star-studded with celebrities from the music and entertainment industries (and artist and philanthropist, Jeff Hanson?). Lady Gaga provided an over-the-top performance to highlight the evening, which basically ended at breakfast.

Julie and I stood in the manicured English gardens with our cocktails, watching Jeff chat with Kelly and Sharon Osbourne. *OK, this is getting a little surreal. We're from Kansas, everybody! Wasn't this kid just sitting at the foot of our driveway, selling water color note cards from a lemonade stand under an umbrella?* Now 16, Jeff worked the crowd, handing out business cards when appropriate, trying to push his artwork for EJAF. He even managed to sell his hand-painted bowtie and cummerbund to someone at our dinner table, with the £1000 profit going to EJAF. *It's time to quit feeling sorry for Jeff. He's found his niche. Elton always said he would. He's having a blast!*

*Art. Philanthropy. Entrepreneurship. Jeff is focusing on what he **can do**, not what he **can't do.***

(And Sir Elton. For taking the time, and having the compassion, generosity and patience to allow an infatuated young fan **see** so much more than a low vision glimpse of a superstar's life, we thank you!)

****

January 25, 2008
To the attention of Sir Elton John:
Elton—
Seeing you again, in Abu Dhabi, was a "sight for sore eyes."
Thank you for the trip of a lifetime! The dinner invitation to your Emirates Palace suite was over-the-top! I never dreamed I would be able to spend so much time with you, and I loved every second of it.
We loved the concert. Mom cried through your dedication of "Circle of Life." Great song with great lyrics.
The following day we toured and shopped Dubai (you were right— much better than Abu Dhabi), before flying out that night. We made it safely home to Kansas City, and I am back at school at the Kansas State School for the Blind on Friday, Jan 25.
I am already planning some "African" themed abstract artwork, for the

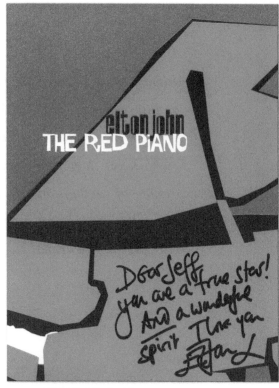

elton john
THE RED PIANO

Dear Jeff
you are a true star!
And a wonderful
spirit Thank you

Julie presented Elton with her signature white chocolate macadamia nut cheesecake, backstage during a visit to Kansas City. Jeff greets Sir Arthur in Las Vegas, November 2012, at Million Dollar Piano. Ready for White Tie and Tiara in Old Windsor, England, June 2010.

EJAF houses in South Africa, and will be in touch about this.

*Although most famous for your musical career, Elton, you now seem to be just as much **"defined by generosity."** Your enormous effort for EJAF is an inspiration to my own fundraising project.*

I will never forget—and will forever cherish—the unprecedented expression of compassion and generosity you have shown a 14-year-old boy from Kansas, who only dreamed......to someday meet Sir Elton John.

With Love and Warmest Regards,

Jeff

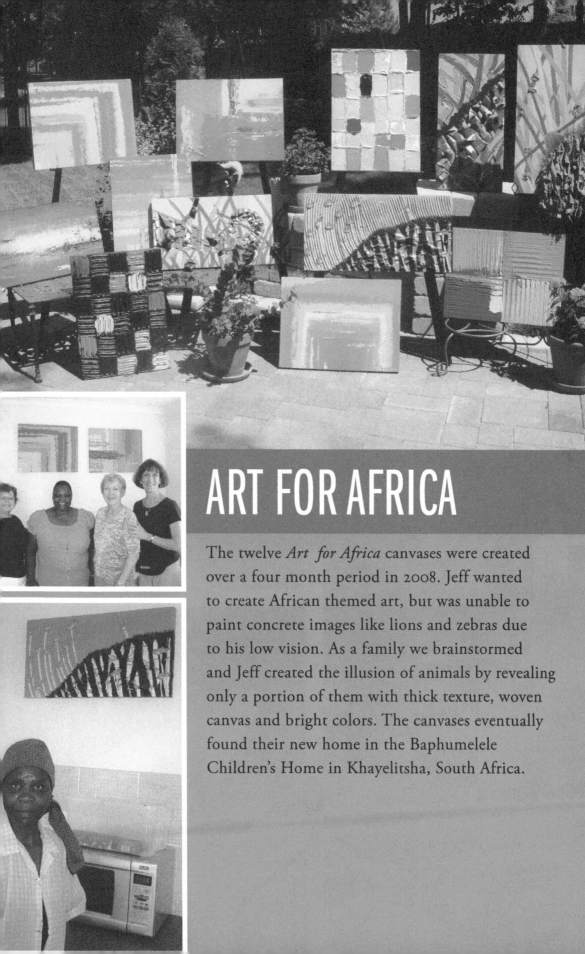

ART FOR AFRICA

The twelve *Art for Africa* canvases were created over a four month period in 2008. Jeff wanted to create African themed art, but was unable to paint concrete images like lions and zebras due to his low vision. As a family we brainstormed and Jeff created the illusion of animals by revealing only a portion of them with thick texture, woven canvas and bright colors. The canvases eventually found their new home in the Baphumelele Children's Home in Khayelitsha, South Africa.

Bye-bye, see you again soon!

BAPHUMELELE
CHILDREN'S HOME

December 29, 2008

Dear Julie and the family,

We really would like to thank Jeffrey for the wonderful paintings donated to us here at baphumelele, this is best present we have ever get, best paintings, we highly appreciate that, he has brought a smile to all the children, they are showing off the best pieces, thank once again.

We were very happy to get you Christmas message on the 24th, we felt blessed and loved, Dear Jeffrey your kind donation has helped us to save young, innocent children, whose lives have all been impacted by the HIV/Aids pandemic rampaging in our country – they are orphans or they have been abandoned by dying parents, they have been dumped as little babies or they are HIV-positive themselves. One way or another, they have all already experienced death, disease, abuse, neglect and hunger in their still so young lives.

It is people like you, who help to give them back their childhood, their smiles, their trust in life and a future. We are very grateful for your support.

All the best,

Rosie Mashale
Managing director

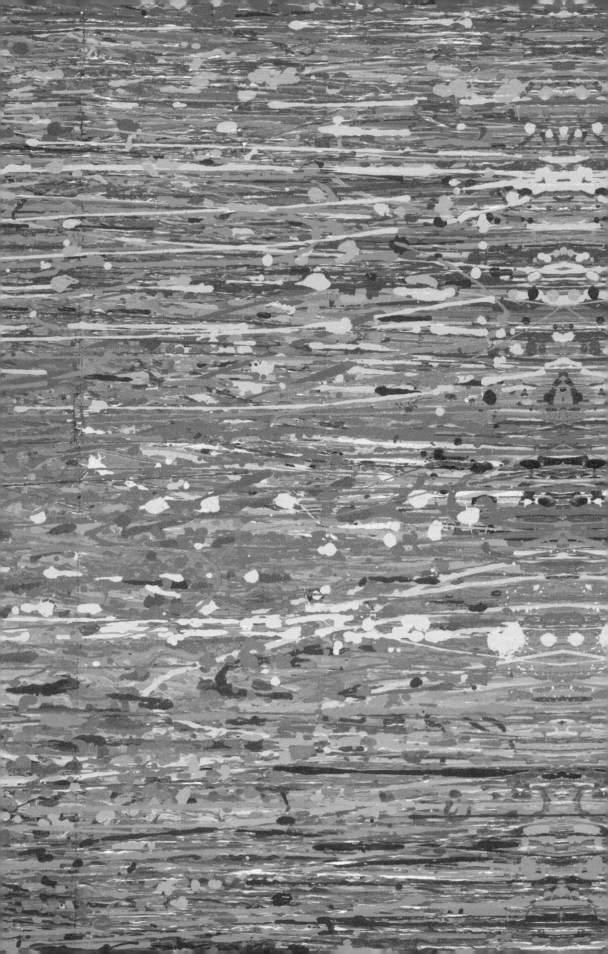

The Accidental Artist

I always knew I wanted to be a doctor. My aunts and uncles would pinch my cheek and ask me what I wanted to be when I grew up. "A doctor," I quickly replied, and they would smile. "Good choice!" From the time I was in third grade, growing up in McCallsburg, Iowa, I admired our family doctor and his small, successful practice. Coming from a large, fairly poor, farming family, I realized the financial security and social status of being a physician, even at that age. I never considered any other career. It had to be medicine. While other kids were outside playing baseball, I was in my room building and painting models of *The Visible Man* and *The Human Heart*. I was determined to become a doctor, and was driven to succeed. Like Scarlet O'Hara, I vowed "as God is my witness, I will never be poor again!"

Jeff never said, "I think I want to be an artist when I grow up." And if he had, his mother and I would have quickly discouraged him. What job security does that offer? Jeff's childhood "career list" included bulldozer operator, chef, cruise boat concierge, and video game tester. He never mentioned art. No one mentioned art. No one knew anything about art. No one had an interest in art. Our parents didn't appreciate art. They couldn't afford it. *Art is for rich people.* I'm a science/biology guy. Julie studied marketing and fashion merchandising. The extent of my art knowledge was that the *Mona Lisa* was old and very expensive. And that was OK, because I didn't like it that much anyway. So even with the best of vision, art was a very unlikely career choice for Jeff. And when his vision failed, an art career seemed laughable.

Jeff's art experience was the same as every other kid. Crayons, coloring books, colored pencils, dot art and water color paints. His creations hung on the refrigerator for a few days and then secretly found their way to the circular file, only to be replaced soon by another spark of genius. He took art class in elementary school, where every kid came home with the identical picture of a cat or a mountain. And when Jeff's vision deteriorated at around age 10, any thought of an art career would have escaped the "dream bank" like so many others.

Even during *Jeff's Bistro*, and the 5000 hand-painted note cards that were sold, no one talked about art as a profession. It was a hobby. Nothing more. And it was "kid art." I didn't appreciate any true artistic talent. *But then, what do I know?*

But I must say he loved it. It was something he could do. Jeff painted almost every day. And with his ADHD, the activity seemed to have a calming effect on him, which he subconsciously recognized. And it allowed him to be creative. He loved to sit and paint and experiment. Neurofibromatosis and low vision did not seem to affect his creativity. Jeff's note cards were high contrast, colorful, abstract, fun and made you smile. But that's all it was. *We thought.*

Kid Art. But you appreciate the inner genius, don't you? The Hindenburg, *(crayon on typing paper),* Grandma's Quilt, *(colored pencil on grocery bag),* Sailing into Monaco on a Tuesday with Teddy, *(crayon—the big 64 box with sharpener—on butcher's paper),* Gibraltar from the Deck of the Santa Maria in 1492 *(acrylic on Kansas sedimentary rock).*

In fact, in 2005, if you would have told me that anyone would actually pay money for a piece of artwork created in our house, I would have laughed. Art was so foreign to our household and upbringing that it was not a consideration.

Some very dear friends of ours were once over for dinner, and Ken commented that "what this house needs is some nice artwork." I just nodded in agreement, not knowing at all what he was talking about. I still liked my faded posters from college. Our home was already artistically perfect. All of our walls were safely painted beige.

So for Jeff, at age 12, to be called an "artist," seemed a bit absurd. He painted note cards at the foot of our driveway, and was called an artist. *The visually impaired artist!* But it was tongue-in-cheek, (at first). *The Kansas City Star* said his "Fundraiser Has Vision," and "For Legally Blind Artist, Life is Outside the Box." But Jeff was not really planning to BE an artist. He didn't think of himself as an artist. This whole "art/note card thing" was about to go away anyway, I thought. It raised a lot of money for charity. It had served its purpose to entertain Jeff, and his parents, through a rough time. That was over, and we were moving on.

I was actually at a loss at that time, as to what Jeff **would** be able to do for a career. He was 12 and attending the Kansas State School for the Blind. Think about it. He had poor coordination and learning disabilities. He struggled to read. As a parent you are constantly trying to steer your child down *the correct path.* I honestly did not know what that path might be, and was hoping his school would guide him in career choice and training, to help him find meaningful work as an adult.

I had run out of dreams long ago.

We credit Jeff's ophthalmologist, Dr. Grin, (love that name, and it suits her well), with the evolution of Jeff's art from note cards to canvas. She had traveled the journey with us. She had attended the "farewell to CLOD" balloon launch. She knew all about *Jeff's Bistro*, and the hand-painted note cards. She even sold them in her office to her patients. She knew Jeff gave the money to charity. And she herself was very philanthropic, donating her time and surgical skills to the Medical Missions Foundation in Kansas City, to provide medical care to indigent children in several countries.

But Dr. Grin had a cataclysmic idea. (Pivotal moment here).

"Jeff, would you be willing to recreate one of your note cards on canvas, and donate the painting to the 'Art for the Children' auction to benefit the Medical Missions Foundation?"

Jeff agreed. But he had never painted anything big before. And he really didn't know how to do it. There were no canvases at our house. I had seen them for sale at hobby stores, and figured we could buy one and help Jeff translate one of his note cards to the larger scale. But Jeff only did this as a favor to his eye doctor. And it was a fun challenge. There was no thought of him being *an artist*. He was just a kid with a passion for art, who played around with paints. Even the invitation to paint was interpreted by me as a kind, compassionate gesture. *Make Jeff feel important. Give him a **purpose**.*

Julie and Jeff shopped for paints and a 30" x 40" canvas, to create the note card enlargement. They chose a card style that they thought would have the broadest appeal. We helped Jeff pencil out the areas of color on the canvas, bringing the note card up to scale. He painted it all with mini-rollers rather than brushes, and indeed he did effectively reproduce the card onto canvas. It was pretty cool,

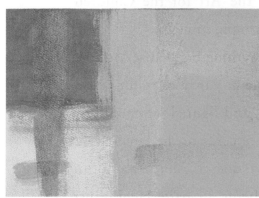

From a 5" x 7" note card, Jeff created the 30" x 40" acrylic on canvas, Visions III, *for his ophthalmologist, Dr. Trudi Grin, shown with Jeff at The Medical Missions Foundation "Art for the Children" Gala. Painted only with mini-rollers, the masterpiece was snatched up by a private collector. You'll see this again on a Sotheby's auction.*

and a lot of fun to create. Jeff was proud of it. But he still wasn't *an artist*. Farthest thing from our minds.

February, 2007. The Medical Missions Foundation Gala was a black tie affair with the usual silent auction, dinner and live auction. Four hundred people. Jeff's painting, *Visions III*, was on the silent auction. I watched like a mouse in the corner to see the reaction of the attendees. This was our version of proud parents going to their kid's soccer game (which the low vision kid would never play). Surprisingly, several people bid on the piece, and it eventually sold for $400. And several of the bidders did not know Jeff's story or that he was a patient of Dr. Grin. I am not even sure they knew he had low vision. *They just bid on it because they liked it?* This was pretty cool. That was easy money. Dr. Grin was right. Jeff was only 13 years old. He was thrilled. Jeff's art generated money for Medical Missions. Generosity and philanthropy continued to define him. But he still wasn't *an artist*.

That was just the beginning of the note-card-to-canvas transformation. Jeff really enjoyed the canvas concept. So we all decided Jeff should do it again—this time to benefit our local church fundraiser. So in May, 2007, he created another 30" x 40" canvas, enlarging another note card. This time he was on stage at a live auction. Sold. $550! But this audience knew Jeff and his story. And it was a very understanding, sympathetic crowd. Not a fair measure of his artistic value. More "pity money?"

Through that summer, Jeff linked up with his former elementary school art teacher, Aimee, and they spent several sessions together, experimenting with art media and techniques. They slashed canvases with razor blades and rewove them with more strips of raw canvas.

They dumped paint off the deck balcony onto canvases below. They mixed sandy grit into paint, textured "goo" onto canvases, and glued all sorts of strange things onto the art. It was a fun, enlightening experience for Jeff that opened his mind to limitless creative concepts. Jeff was truly taking a serious interest in art.

But then, in September, 2007, a curious thing happened. Jeff was contacted by a couple who had seen his work at the Medical Missions Foundation Gala several months prior. They were out-bid on his piece that night, but remembered his story, and art, and wanted to *commission* Jeff to create something for them on canvas! *They would just PAY HIM for his art? Are you kidding me? There is a lot of art out there, folks, are you sure this is what you want?*

Generosity begets generosity.

They wanted Jeff to create some artwork for them because they liked his bold colors, and *they loved his STORY* of philanthropy, and finding his way through adversity. They didn't want to buy artwork that didn't have a story behind it. (*OK…make a mental note of that*).

It's not the challenge, but our **response** to the challenge that defines us.

This "commission" concept wasn't totally foreign to Jeff. He had created a few other canvases from note cards by this time. But those were only for friends and neighbors. This couple—these people—were perfect strangers! And they sought Jeff out for his artwork! This idea excited Jeff, and reinforced his passion for painting. **People liked his artwork!**

I'm not sure how we ever agreed upon a price. Jeff was 14 years old. He had never put a price on his art. Not really. Friends and neighbors would negotiate a fair price based on cost of materials, and time spent. And his art, by my description, up to this point, was "kid art." But now people were telling us, "no, it's not!" This couple combed through Jeff's large "portfolio" *(dare I even use that word? Isn't that what artists have?)* of old note cards, and selected one to be enlarged onto canvas. Jeff created a really fun, predominantly red painting that seemed to please his customers. And they paid him for it! Cold cash. U.S. dollars. Money for Jeff's savings account. (And a small deposit into my dream bank).

This whole experience would require some pondering.

We decided as a family that Jeff should take on a project that was more ambitious. The idea was to create a series of six 30" x 30" canvases that hung together as a group. Julie and Jeff went through his archives of note cards (the *portfolio*--we had saved back examples of all his previous note card styles), and chose six that seemed to work together. They were all painted in screaming hot colors, with bold bands of other colors swiped across them. The canvases were created all at once, laid out across our basement floor. They were big, startling, happy and really got your attention.

But the art work needed a title. Jeff was now naming all of his pieces. And we photographed each one to keep a record for future reference. Jeff thought they were a "sight for sore eyes!"

"What did you just say?"

"They're a sight for sore eyes."

Thunderclap! They **were** a sight for sore eyes! They were beautiful, and pleasing to the eye. And they showed us the world—Jeff's abstract interpretation of the world—through his "sore eyes."

Perfect! The title was perfect! It was more than perfect. Meant to be. And the expression became a tag line for Jeff's art.

The six canvas series, *Sight for Sore Eyes*, was displayed in our church coffee shop. It later sold for $2400 to Ransom Memorial Hospital in Ottawa, Kansas, to become the décor of their new conference center. The hospital had been looking for some art that "had a **story** to it." Jeff kept half the money to cover expenses, and gave half to charity.

The kid's hobby was making him some money, and it was fun. He could really do it! But wasn't this just like any other kid doing part-time odd jobs? Mowing lawns. Bagging groceries. Working the fast food drive-through. Jeff never planned to keep doing it as an adult. It never occurred to him. Not as a career.

Commissions began to escalate after that. People who had seen *Sight for Sore Eyes* displayed at our church coffee shop began coming over to our home to see Jeff's work, watch him paint and order pieces for themselves. Charitable foundations heard about the philanthropic, low vision kid who painted and donated to "charities that had touched his life." Kid's charities, like Make-A-Wish Foundation, Children's Mercy Hospital in Kansas City, (where Jeff received treatment), The Elton John AIDS Foundation, the Children's Tumor Foundation, and Medical Missions Foundation all benefitted from Jeff's generosity.

A large, local apartment complex, in the process of a total make-over, approached Jeff to design artwork for their lobby and all of their signage and marketing. They want Jeff Hanson! I was speechless. Their interior designers had seen Jeff's art and selected it as the inspiration for their remodel. *They simply loved his art!*

Painting canvases became more than a hobby—it became a **passion**. A passion both for the art, and for philanthropy.

Jeff began offering paintings to more "live" charity auctions.

September 2007. Clients Boris and Lisa select
their note card inspiration, and later pose with
the completed work. Boulevard Apartments
redecorated their reception area around Jeff's
commissioned Boulevard Brights. People
actually liked Jeff's artwork, and were willing
to pay money for it.

Since most of these functions were black tie events, Jeff adopted the "tuxedo look" as his trademark. But Jeff added a twist. The cummerbund and bow tie that he wore with his tux were hand-painted by Jeff, to match the artwork being auctioned. And to heighten the bidding war, Jeff would offer to "throw those in" for the winning bidder.

November, 2008. Jeff first tested his tuxedo "brand" at a live auction gala for Angel Flight, an organization that arranges free air transportation by volunteer pilots, to fly ill children to their medical treatments. Jeff donated a large canvas, and wore matching bow tie and cummerbund. The canvas, *High Altitude*, sold for $2000, and Jeff also told the audience he would create and donate a second painting if the runner-up bidder agreed to give Angel Flight another $2000. Sold! This was fun, and easy, and it felt great to stand on stage and be so generous. *He may not really be an artist, but he certainly was becoming a philanthropist. At age 15.*

New Year's Eve, 2008. The Kansas City Make-A-Wish Foundation's New Year's Eve Gala. Jeff, the 15-year-old philanthropic, former Make-A-Wish kid, was a natural to be live on stage, in a tuxedo, encouraging the bidding. Who could resist? His splattered blue-on-silver triptych, *Sky's the Limit*, went for $600. Jeff had a blast! The live auctions were becoming a lot of fun. It became a challenge to create art and see how high the bidding would go on auction.

Jeff funded all of this himself. Mom and dad's wallet never provided anything more than those first few canvases and paints from the hobby store. The proceeds from commissioned paintings easily covered his cost of supplies for donated works.

Jeff created 106 original paintings on canvas in 2008. He gifted 15 of those to people who had "touched his life." Another 23 were donated to charitable events, for auction. The remaining 68 were commissions for profit. The after-school job was keeping him very busy. And it was meaningful, gratifying work for the 15-year-old, low vision kid who couldn't catch a ball or ride a bike. He could do it, and do it well. And with practice and repetition, the art gradually became more complex, sophisticated and intriguing. *Was this an artist?*

Focus on what you **can** do, not what you **can't**.

The year 2009 was even more astounding. Jeff painted 257 canvases, with substantial gifts to charitable live auctions and foundations. He had his first ever, sole-artist exhibition in the Kansas City Crossroads Arts District, generating thousands for our local Children's Mercy Hospital, as well as Elton's Baphumelele Children's Home in South Africa. Events like that give you clout, and credibility—*as an artist?* And validation for your prices. Mom kept a log-book documenting Jeff's gifts to charity, and what his paintings sold for on charitable auctions.

Clout and credibility continued to build.

The new "aLOFT Hotel" in Leawood, KS, searched the Kansas City art market, seeking a local artist to be featured at their grand opening in October, 2009. Their research committee selected Jeffrey Owen Hanson. They had seen some of his paintings that were displayed at a local gallery. *They simply loved his art!*

But was Jeff really an *artist?* He started to acknowledge that he was, because everyone around him kept calling him one. He just went along with it. So did his parents. He never really planned to be an artist. He never trained to be an artist. Being an artist requires innate talent, years of study and training at an art school, eccentricity,

New Year's Eve 2008. Make-A-Wish Gala in K.C. The tuxedo brand becomes a trademark.
Jeff went on to show his work at several local galleries, and sold a lot of paintings to
customers who did not know about his visual impairment or story.

failure, and yes, **starvation**. Then you can call yourself an artist. You've earned the title.

Jeff hadn't gone down that road. He initially saw himself as a kid with art as a hobby, and a heart for philanthropy. The real passion for art as a career came later, slowly evolving with encouragement and positive feedback from his clients.

No art critic ever critiqued him. No juried art show ever judged him. No one from the art world ever recognized him. Jeff didn't even know what any of those things were. But his clients couldn't get enough of him.

Jeff says art just happened to be the vehicle that got him in the "philanthropic limelight." It could have been anything—sports, writing, theater, music, baking apple pies—if he could have done those things. Art just happened to be **what he could do**, given the circumstances. So he did it. And the more he did it, the better it got. *Focus on what you* ***can*** *do.* People kept calling him an artist, so he just went along with it. Unlikely, yes. Unintentional, yes. The accidental artist.

I suppose there are many people out there in "accidental" careers, with unintended consequences. I sincerely doubt that Steve Jobs realized where his garage electronics tinkering would lead. His hobby and interests eventually led him into a career field. Did billionaire Warren Buffett dare to dream of his future position and career? If he did, that man had quite a "dream bank!"

But take your average business person or entrepreneur. They have an idea, or invent a product, that eventually takes off. They accidently land on something that makes them highly successful. The Hula Hoop craze in the 50's? Google? Facebook? The Snuggie? Who would have thought? All of them "accidental careers." Jeff's just happened to be art. He "tinkered with art." And his creativity, story and philanthropy permitted him to become successful with it.

There never was a day when Jeffrey Owen Hanson said, "I want to be an artist." Or, "I guess I'm an artist." It just gradually happened, unintentionally, accidently, and we all grew to accept it.

****

Kansas City Internal Medicine is a large medical practice with multiple offices around the metro area. They have commissioned multiple pieces of artwork from Jeff to decorate their waiting areas. His artwork is perfect for public and corporate spaces like that. Large, bright, abstract, happy art. Provocative. Heavily textured. Electric colors. Art with wonderment. Art with a story.

Sitting in one of those waiting rooms myself one day, I overheard this conversation between two patients.

"I just love the artwork they have here."

The other patient looked up and studied the paintings for a few seconds. "Oh, yes, those are Jeff Hanson's. I would know his work anywhere. Very unique style."

Jeff was 16.

*I guess Jeff is **an artist!***

SIGHT FOR SORE EYES

Bold, huge and risky for the young artist, the six canvases were a relatively large investment of time, money and creativity. The series solidly established Jeff's style with the 2.5" deep canvases painted on all edges, blazing colors and bold signature. Nothing about them was timid or subtle— advantages of low vision. This was the first time we clearly saw the world through Jeff's "sore eyes."

Hospital CEO Larry Felix poses with Jeff in front of Sight for Sore Eyes, *in the new hospital conference center.*

Building A
Business Backwards

If Jeff Hanson is the accidental artist, Jeffrey Owen Hanson LLC is the accidental business.

At the conclusion of *Jeff's Bistro* in the Fall of 2006, Jeff closed the driveway bake sale and art store forever. The multicolored umbrella was put away. That was the end. There were no plans for any further fundraisers, bistro's or artwork. Remember, he wasn't an *artist*. Only the hand-painted note cards were continued—just for fun. All three of us thought Jeff would just go back to seventh grade at the Kansas State School for the Blind, and try to return to "normalcy." We never talked about plans for any more art or charity work. We could just relax a bit, after our big bump in the road.

Looking back now, I can't imagine life had we followed that course. We could have chosen to do nothing more. (Pivotal moment). No canvases. No charities. No auctions. No philanthropy. No art customers. No paintings taking over our entire basement. Life back to how it was in 2005? What would we have done with ourselves? We are three (maybe two and a half), driven, type-A, never sleep, anal, neurotics! (*And proud of it!*) We all would have gone stir crazy! There is a limit to what a low vision kid can do for jobs and entertainment. Jeff can't drive a car. Everyone at his former school was playing sports all summer. Not Jeff's forté. And you can only watch so much TV.

Fortunately for Jeff, and his parents, the art *business* did not stop there. Customers continued to come to us, seeking Jeff's art *and story*. They wanted to know all about CLOD, *Jeff's Bistro*, Elton John and Dubai. They wanted to see how a low vision kid paints, and where he gets his inspiration. They wanted to join the band wagon and support Jeff's favorite charities like Make-A-Wish and the Children's Tumor Foundation. They wanted to hug Jeff and become part of his story. They wouldn't allow him to quit. Public outcry! His fans demanded more.

And we didn't say, "No, we don't do that anymore."

One by one, Jeff agreed to create another painting for this person, or that charity auction, never intending to do this indefinitely. And it was fun. And rewarding, both financially and for self-esteem. Just one more. And another. And another. A little more spending money. Jeff's after-school activity.

Thinking back, when Jeff started losing his vision in 2003, I had regretted that I wasn't in another career besides medicine. I wished we had a family business that Jeff would be able to join as an adult. It was problem enough that he had neurofibromatosis and learning difficulties. Add low vision to the formula, and good jobs become limited. But if we had a family-owned business—a dry cleaners, a restaurant, a retail store—Jeff could walk right into a position once he graduated from high school. It wouldn't matter that he couldn't drive a car, or read fluently. We would find a place for him in the business.

But as an ER doctor, there was no way to introduce Jeff into *my business*. He was going to have to find his own career. And that really concerned his mother and I. We had no time, resources, knowledge or emotional energy to start up a family business in addition to my medical career. It was all we could juggle just to get Jeff through his medical treatments, his education and our day to day lives.

(Busí ness) The occupation, work, or trade in which a person is engaged. Commercial, industrial or professional dealings; the buying and selling of commodities or services.

Technically speaking, even *Jeff's Bistro* in 2006 was a business. A family business. No one thought of it quite that way. There were no licenses, permits or tax ID numbers. It was a fun summer pastime, and charity fundraiser. But Jeff did engage in commercial dealings with customers, sell commodities (note cards and brownies), and accept money in trade for goods. We all helped. He did not generate any profits, because he gave all the *Bistro* proceeds to charity. In fact, most of his customers wrote their checks directly to the Children's Tumor Foundation, so Jeff did not have to claim any income or file a tax return.

But the seeds of a family business were unknowingly planted in *Jeff's Bistro,* and the ideas that sprouted from them on art, philanthropy and entrepreneurship slowly began to grow. No one noticed it at first. No one had time for a family business (*we thought*). No one was trained or ready for this. But the three of us were incubating and nurturing these seedlings, and they were about to break ground.

First signs of life appeared in 2008. For starters, in January, Julie and Jeff decided Jeff needed to create a website. It wasn't really intended to market artwork, or be linked to any type of *business*. It was initially an informational site, telling Jeff's story, and helping people find hope and inspiration in the midst of their own adversity. It encouraged positive thinking, generosity and philanthropy. I didn't see why we needed to spend money creating a website like that, but Jeff and Julie felt it could motivate others to focus on "what they **can do**, rather than dwelling on what they **can't**." The website was created, and Jeff paid for it with half-cash, and half-bartering. The web designer liked Jeff's artwork so much that he agreed to swap half his fee for some original artwork for his office. (Now this was an interesting concept).

The website turned out great, and started getting lots of hits. Many were simply "attaboy" comments, but several were prospective *clients* curious about his art, and wondering how they might obtain a piece. I really don't know how people found Jeff, or what drove them to his site. He wasn't <u>linked</u> to any other site. Possibly they sought Jeff out after seeing him on stage at a live auction, in a tuxedo. But here we go. I started to notice that if you "Googled" Jeff, his name was moving up the suggested list. It wasn't long before if you typed "Jeffrey," he was number two. (Right behind serial killer Jeffrey Dahmer—a little disturbing).

The next thing I noticed in 2008 was that Jeff never seemed to be "caught up" with his canvas painting. He constantly had commissions pending, with deadlines for completion. There was never a break. A good problem to have, even for a *non-business*. In fact, from March of 2008 to the time of this writing, Jeff has *never caught up on commissions!* He is usually three or four months behind. His mother was, and is, always on the run, ordering canvases and supplies to keep the production line moving.

And hand-painted note cards still hadn't gone away. In fact, they were getting out of control again. A decision was made to take some of Jeff's favorite card styles to a printing company and have them mass-produced. We were all reluctant to do this, because hand-painted cards are very special. They are unique. No one sells them. But they were just too labor intensive to continue. And they were taking over our house everywhere, drying, and being pressed flat.

Two sets of six note cards were printed in 2008, and were sold through the website. "Jeff's Favorites" and "Sight for Sore Eyes" were marketed, with all proceeds going to charity. Later came "Art for Africa," the Elton John AIDS Foundation canvases photographed and printed on note cards to benefit EJAF. That ended the note card production at home, and freed up more time for original art on canvas.

But the most significant thing of all about 2008 was that Jeff's *non-business, business* was starting to turn a profit! It wasn't all about charity. He was earning some spending money, too. I didn't pay much attention to it at first. It was like lawn-mowing or babysitting money. As a parent, who really keeps track? But toward the end of the year, as the sales stacked up, I questioned Jeff about how much money he thought he had made that year. Jeff really didn't know. He had lots of expenses, purchasing paint and canvases. And he gave many of the paintings away instead of selling them for profit. But still, it seemed to me he was doing more *business* than a teenage baby sitter. So after a little investigating of receipts from the hobby store,

The home page of the original website, which was only intended to tell Jeff's story and inspire others. Note cards arrive from the printer. The burden and mess of hand-painted note cards all over the house was lifted. But then came the job of order fulfillment from the website. All proceeds from note card sales went to charity.

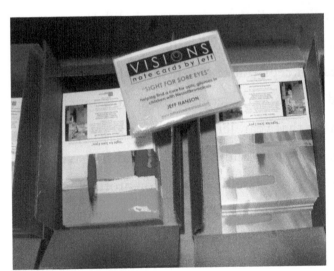

and deposits into his savings account, his mother and I realized *this kid needs to file taxes!* Jeff had gross sales of $35,000! Yikes! He was 15 years old, for Pete's sake! Subtracting out all the *business* expenses and deductions that a 15-year-old can take, Jeff paid taxes on $9,400. He filed as the "sole proprietor" of his *business*.

Which brought up a great opportunity. I had known for years that Jeff needed to start an IRA. With low vision and a questionable visual future, he needed to be socking money away and let the magic of compounding do its work. But he never had any significant earned income. He had never filed income tax before. You have to report your earnings to the IRS in order to qualify for an IRA. But now, finally!

The key here is "time." Nobody's retirement plan starts growing at age fifteen. You're lucky if you are 25, or even 35, and are depositing into a retirement plan. Those extra 10 or 20 years tacked on to the beginning of your savings period can do amazing things. Plugging $5,000 per year into a Roth IRA starting at age 15, earning a modest 5% average interest, growing for 50 years till Jeff is 65, is worth a whopping $1,104,000. (Might only buy a loaf of bread in the year 2060, but still sounds fantastic). If it had *only* grown for 40 years (still a long time for a retirement plan), its value is $639,000. Run to the bank as fast as you can!

With the increasing art sales in 2008, I now saw an opportunity for Jeff to start a Roth IRA. And he agreed. Selling a few paintings every year would allow him the *employment* he needed at a young age to make deposits for his retirement. Jeff found the whole concept very intriguing. He was curious about how to invest the money, and explored options with our family financial planner. (And, oh yes,

Warren Buffett! Keep reading).

But then came another hurdle. SALES TAX! We knew nothing about this. Our 15-year-old son needs to be charging his art customers sales tax? And report it to the State of Kansas? He's just a kid. Do we really have to do this? I'm an ER doctor. I work for a hospital and get a W-2 at the end of the year. Doctor's don't charge sales tax. I don't know how to compute and file sales tax.

In February of 2009, I called up the State of Kansas Department of Revenue, to get some information. I was just sure kids didn't have to do this. It went like this.

"*Your business* needs to collect and pay 8.65% sales tax, quarterly, on all sales in the State of Kansas. How long have you been in business?"

"Beats me! I didn't even know we had a business!"

"What date will you use to begin filing from?"

"Hmmmmm. Excellent question."

"What was the date of your first sale?"

"I'll have to look that up."

"Do you have a business?"

"I'm not sure yet."

"I see."

Did I come off sounding unprofessional? Ignorant? We don't really have a business, do we? What I have learned, over and over, is that when in doubt, GOOGLE!! And after some internet research, I learned that indeed Jeff **did** need to be reporting and paying sales tax to Topeka, and we were already delinquent on our sales taxes!

I just picked a date. April 1, 2008. Yep. That's the day we decided to start up an art business. I remember it well. The celebration. The fanfare. The ribbon cutting. The pageantry of it all! Our family art

Caught sleeping on the job, Jeff's photographer neglected to do a photo shoot of the first official day of business, April 1, 2008. We only have our waning memories of that celebrated, historic day. Dad's ER lab coats were recycled by Jeff into artful painter's smocks.

business was born. What a day to remember! (*The one thing we don't have photos of*).

I scrounged up receipts and bank records and surmised that the most likely date that we started to own a family business was April 1, 2008. Maybe. Approximately. But don't most people know if they own a business? We didn't. Jeff never said, "Let's start an art business." No one said it. But we had one. The State of Kansas said so.

It crept into our lives like a fog.

No wonder I couldn't get anything done! OMG! We had an art business! I wondered where all my time was going. Julie felt the same way. And Jeff's life was school, homework, paint. School, homework, paint. No wonder! We owned a family business! *Hey, everybody, we have an art business!* We didn't know!!

I was the director of an emergency department, and I owned a family business on the side. (Actually, Jeff owned an art business, but the State of Kansas made me sign the papers as *owner*, since Jeff was a minor).

I was a scattered mess! So was Julie. We had partially completed projects lying around everywhere. Everything was half-done (not even half). At work and at home. I suddenly had ADD, bouncing from fire to fire, touching anything shiny, never quite completing anything around the house. But Julie and I were helping Jeff constantly. It seemed minor at first. It sneaks up on you. Like helping your kid with a school science project. But it slowly snowballed into endless chores. Shopping for art supplies. Talking to clients. Photographing canvases. Moving canvases too large for one person to move. Varnishing. Creating all sorts of new mixed-media techniques with wires, ropes and torn strips of canvas. Filing taxes.

And more taxes. Setting up accounting books. Website maintenance. Computer glitches. Answering a steady stream of emails inquiring about art. Billing. Shipping. You name it!

I had to go back nine months, and file three quarters of sales tax returns for 2008. (With penalty). It seems quite fitting that the business' glorious "grand opening" was on April **Fool's** Day! Fortunately, "type-A" family members had all the receipts. But I never took a business or accounting class in my life, and neither did Julie. Figuring out those returns was a challenge. I immediately sought help from a professional small business tax accountant, Joe, who has since rescued me from the depths of hell on a quarterly basis.

Jeff's sole proprietorship became an LLC a year later, on April 1, 2009, at our accountant's suggestion (April Fool's, again). Julie became Jeff's first salaried employee on April 1, 2011 (seems to be a theme, here). Jeff's signature was soon trademarked, and he was looking more and more like a real business man.

Throughout all of this, Jeff's health condition remained stable. What we feared—progressive vision loss—never developed. To the surprise of Jeff's medical team and his parents, Jeff's vision made gradual **improvement** from 2006 to 2009. The radiation therapy directed toward CLOD worked better than expected. A lot better. Jeff's vision stabilized at 20/80, in patchy spots in his visual fields, and remained there. Jeff could slowly read two or three lines below the "big E" on the vision chart, which was dramatically better than pre-radiation. And with improved vision, came improved art work. Partly from frying CLOD, partly from maturity and gradual adaptation, and partly a "GOD-THING," we all celebrated the vision that was now preserved.

And remarkably, after three and a half years at the Kansas State School for the Blind and the completion of ninth-grade, a decision was made to transfer back to a more main-stream school. Jeff had learned Braille and received lots of training in activities of daily living in the low vision world. He had maximized the benefits of the curriculum at KSSB. The threat of progressive blindness into adulthood never materialized. His vision was patchy and poor, but stable.

After researching area high schools, a decision was made to not return to our large public school. Jeff was now accustomed to the atmosphere of a small, quiet school, with small classroom size and lots of one-on-one teaching. We decided as a family to enroll Jeff at Horizon Academy in the fall of 2009, a private area school that specialized in learning disabilities. They were able to accommodate Jeff's low vision, and provided the small school climate Jeff wanted. The decision was a great one, and Jeff loved the transition to high school there. Horizon Academy became Jeff's school until his graduation in May of 2012.

****

Search the web and you will discover endless advice on how to start up your own successful business. "Choose an idea you understand and believe in—what you do best. Find your niche—your focused, target audience for your product and service. Be different. Be smart! Be innovative. Be fast, smile, say thank you, make a good first impression. Be consistent, listen to your customer's feedback, and maintain high quality products and superior service." Sounds so easy.

All this advice assumes that you "A. want a business, and B. actually decided to start one." You then develop your idea—your product or service that you plan to market to your "niche" audience.

What we have learned is that your product must be special—a unique, valued product. It has to have both characteristics. Unique is not enough. A grilled cheese sandwich with a mysterious image resembling the Virgin Mary toasted onto its surface is unique. But valued? A single bar of solid gold bullion is valued, but unique? They all look the same.

Jeff had a unique, valued product. His art work. We didn't know this at the time. Not in 2008. None of us realized how **unique** it was, since we were three artistic illiterates. Jeff's customers had to tell us, over and over, until we started to accept it. We just assumed everyone was painting like this. And the **value** was driven by customer demand. Jeff's prices began to climb, both at charity auctions and his commissioned works for sale. People sought him out. He couldn't keep up with demand, and prices rose accordingly. The public wanted his unique, valued product.

But building Jeff's business to manufacture and market this unique, valued product didn't follow any of the guidelines I found on the internet. Jeff and his parents did it totally backwards. We somehow managed to get it right in the end (all precincts not reporting in on this yet), but getting there gave new meaning to the word *haphazard*. It was, quite literally, **the blind leading the blind!**

For starters, you would think that one of your *business* goals was to make money. Seems logical. But *Jeff's Bistro* was different. Once the black leather chair fell out of the sky and landed on our driveway, the *Bistro* was not-for-profit. Jeff gave all the money away. Businesses can't start up that way. Philanthropy comes later, after the business turns a profit and has taken care of number one. Then they start giving back, if they so choose.

Art display at local Dean & Deluca, for the holidays, 2008. Proceeds went to charity.
Jeff donated a canvas to the Children's Tumor Foundation Gala in New York City, a fundraiser
for neurofibromatosis research. While in New York, he visited Scott P. Campbell, Executive Director
of the Elton John AIDS Foundation and gifted art work to decorate their offices.

Most successful businesses today boast some type of philanthropic endeavor. Check any company's website and you'll learn all about their generosity to charity, and their funding of "green" projects. Save our planet. Hug a tree. It's just good for business. The public loves it. But you can't start out that way—not exclusively.

Jeff's **philanthropy-first** model was unusual, to say the least. Even when he started painting canvases instead of note cards, he gave them to auction fundraisers and charities. He rarely sold a painting at first. His business started out giving everything away, and then when it became more successful, Jeff started keeping some of the profits for himself.

Admittedly, Jeff lived in an "artificial economy." Being a teenager and living at home with his parents provided him with all the food, shelter, clothing and *iTunes* cards he could want. He could afford the luxury of giving all his business profits away. (But what teenager does that?) His business revenue did not have to pay the rent.

But in reality, most small businesses start up in an artificial economy. In the garage, in the basement, or at the computer—the business in born. But not during *working hours!* There is usually a "day job" going on, to support the incubating business. And the old adage, "don't quit your day job," has long been good advice to entrepreneurs tinkering with a new formula for "ceiling wax." Dad's medical "day job" was supporting the invisible family art business (albeit minimally).

This philanthropy-first model, however, had incredible unintended consequences. Even though there was no plan for a family art business at the time, or financial profit, Jeff standing on stage at a charity fundraiser, in a tuxedo, wearing a hand-painted bow tie and cummerbund, inadvertently marketed and branded him as the *philanthropic artist*. At age 15. It gave him credibility, notoriety and perceived value, which promoted his unique, valued products. It was free advertising in front of a captive audience filled with generous, philanthropic people. Thousands of potential art customers, hungry for just a piece of the low vision kid's art and philanthropic story. Jeff didn't plan this. (This concept is not new. Most corporations expect their charitable donations to be publicized and create positive public image, and increased revenue in the end. "Strategic philanthropy," they call it. Even in the mid 1800's, the controversial American businessman, P. T. Barnum, intentionally used philanthropy to market his business ventures. Jeff stumbled onto it unknowingly. *You da man, P.T.*).

Strategic Business Plan. I had never seen those three words put together before. Sounds like some sort of secret military operation. Like Strategic Air Command. Julie said we needed one. She had done her research and business networking around Kansas City, and found the right people to help us. Jeff and I went along with it. We had no idea what she was talking about. Summer 2011 was spent in several sessions at Johnson County Community College, hammering out Jeff's strategic business plan with Sally and Elisa. In the end, it was well worth it.

Jeff was a junior in high school at Horizon Academy, and it was time to make plans for college and a career. College would be difficult with low vision and learning problems. And to what end? What degree? What career? Jeff's art business was already quite successful, (wildly successful, in fact), though "sans strategy." He was on target to sell $140,000 in art that year, at age 17, not to mention generate another $200,000 for charity with canvas donations. College was starting to look a little silly. At least for the time being. We knew too many college graduates coming back home with a diploma, but no job, after four (make that five) years. If Jeff stopped his business now and went to college, he would lose all his momentum. But if Jeffrey Owen Hanson LLC was going to support Jeff as an adult, without parental help, then we needed to solidify a few things to make it happen. The strategic business planning could accomplish that.

Most of the terms were foreign to all of us. Five P's of marketing? Systems and processes? The business model? I didn't see how perfect strangers were going to help us write a business plan when **we** didn't know where we were headed. How can anyone tell you your plan when you are clueless? But in the end, we did come up with a plan. And most importantly, the business plan helped us clearly define where we were, our strengths and weaknesses, and what to do about them. It established beyond a shadow of a doubt that we had a business, in fact a highly successful one, and that we needed to take control of it before it crashed.

And paramount for Jeff was that the business become sustainable over the long term. Not just a novelty that wore off. Jeff ran the risk of fading away as he became an adult, like so many "cute" child movie stars. He would no longer be the pathetic chemotherapy kid. His story couldn't carry him forever. He needed to establish himself as an adult who was not dependent on his childhood story for continued success. (*This is still a work in progress*). Now his story was about art and philanthropy—not pediatric illness.

In the midst of strategic planning, *People* magazine called. Are you kidding me? That was nice timing! Always great for the "P" that

The People photo shoot. An amazing moment, watching your child be photographed for a national magazine. And be defined by generosity. Major deposit for the dream bank.

stands for Promotion! They wanted to do a spot on Jeff for their feature, *Heroes Among Us*. Not so much about his art. It was about his philanthropy. He got a full page spread in the July 18, 2011 issue. We were on our family vacation when it hit the newsstands. Contacts on Jeff's website nearly blew up our laptop. I read and reread that page from *People*. Now Jeff was a "hero." National attention— for this peculiar little non-business, business.

Very peculiar, it was. Jeff didn't know he had a unique, valued product. He didn't plan to start a business. The State of Kansas told us we had a business, and we were still dubious. We don't know when it started. We filed our sales taxes a year late. The business began with a philanthropy-first model, with profit later. The strategic business plan was not developed until after the business was wildly successful. The whole country knew about it. The low vision kid, who really just wanted a leather chair for his room, was now the proud owner and CEO of Jeffrey Owen Hanson LLC, the business built backwards!

****

March 2012. Just before high school graduation. Jeff opened the morning mail and studied a letter. He handed me the large manila envelope and its contents.

"What is this? What does this mean?" The font was too small for Jeff to read.

I took the letter and read. With it was another piece of paper. It was a certificate. An award, really. I stared at the words. I looked at the envelope to make sure it was addressed to us. No, there was no mistake. Jeffrey Owen Hanson. It said it, right there.

"This means…(I hesitated)…this means you have done something very well. Very "right." I stared at the letter again.

"What did I do that was so great?"

"Well, that's a good question."

What did he do that was so great? Why was I holding this piece of paper in my hand? Why us? How did all of this happen?

My dreams all flew out the window, remember? Six years ago. I didn't have any more dreams. Zero balance in the dream bank. I had given up.

I wasn't sure Jeff deserved this. I wasn't sure he had lost sleep enough, perspired enough, created enough, worried enough, suffered enough, or starved enough to earn this. Not yet. I could imagine Steve Jobs opening this letter, when he was 18 years old. Or Facebook's Mark Zuckerberg. Google's Larry Page and Sergey Brin. Alexander Graham Bell. Galileo. Some caveman named Bork who invented the wheel. But not Jeff. Not yet, anyway.

"The United States Small Business Administration has selected Jeffrey Owen Hanson as the 2012 Region VII Young Entrepreneur of the Year."

Jeff's business built backwards.

It's not the challenge, but rather your **response** to the challenge that defines you.

What I thought was so fragile—so broken—so hopeless—continued to amaze me. The shattered vase was now reassembled into a beautiful mosaic sculpture.

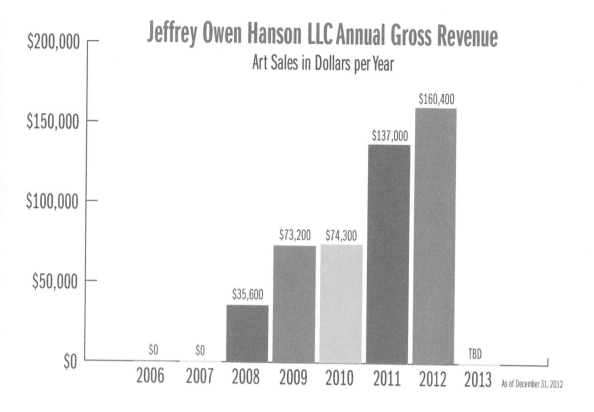

Jeffrey Owen Hanson LLC Annual Gross Revenue
Art Sales in Dollars per Year

As of December 31, 2012

Year	Revenue
2006	$0
2007	$0
2008	$35,600
2009	$73,200
2010	$74,300
2011	$137,000
2012	$160,400
2013	TBD

You can see why the State of Kansas said the kid needed to file sales tax. And why, after High School graduation from Horizon Academy in May 2012, heading off to college was a little questionable. College will still be there in ten years. Will this? Jeff posed with Kansas City, Missouri, Mayor Sly James, after receiving his Young Entrepreneur of the Year 2012 Award.

OPENING NIGHT

One of Jeff's largest canvases of 2009, *Opening Night* was a gift to the Kansas City Art Institute's auction to create scholarships for art students. Jeff at age 16, didn't really consider himself to be a serious artist or plan to attend art school, but helped raise money for those who wanted to pursue careers in art. The 72" x 48" canvas was a very complex, multi-layered, highly textured cityscape, featuring about 75 colors and his "looking through grasses" disguise.

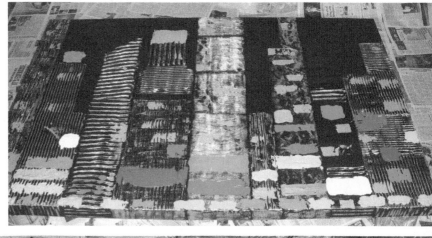
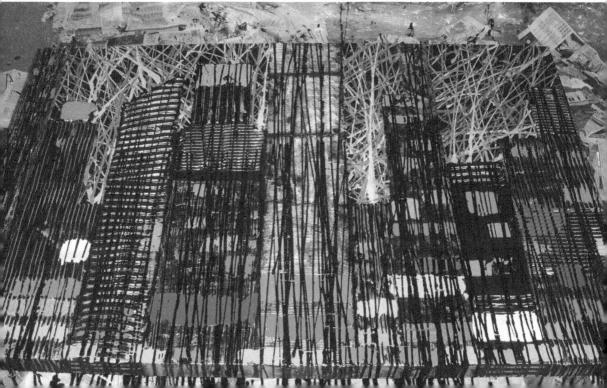

OBSERVATIONS

On Art

Visits to the Hermitage in St. Petersburg, the Louvre in Paris, New York's Museum of Modern Art, and Chicago's Art Institute reveal astounding diversity in what people refer to as "great art." From magnificent da Vinci's to Michelangelo to Monet—the obvious gifts of these virtuosos is unquestionable. The ability of some human beings to translate their world into sculpture or onto canvas is breathtaking. It doesn't seem humanly possible. It's as if they had a digital camera and inkjet printer 400 years ago.

Then there are artists, equally famous, whose talents are less obvious to the untrained, casual observer (observers like Jeff and his parents). Picasso, Warhol, even van Gogh. Their art can be fun, cool, provocative—even disturbing. But the average observer just doesn't see the breathtaking part. Still, their works hang in the world's finest museums and have been crowned "genius" by art critics in the know. A critic's trained eye and understanding and appreciation of "fine art" can quickly discern which artists are truly worthy of the *genius* status.

Self-portrait charcoal, Jeff and Chan, *Fall 2005, at age 12, before chemotherapy. The sketch was much larger than this, reduced here for printing.*

And finally, there are artists, again acclaimed for their creativity and vision, where the average Joe will just stand in front of their work and say, "I don't get it." Or, "I could have done that!" Take a look at the Russian Kazimir Malevich's *Black Square* or *White on White*, as examples.

(fine art) usually referring to a visual art form created for aesthetic purposes and judged for its beauty and meaningfulness.

But I have to be careful what I say here. This chapter shouldn't even be in this book. We have no business commenting on what is good and what is bad about art. I can't even draw a stick man. And we don't want to shoot ourselves in the foot. Jeff is trying to make a few bucks, too, in this world of art we know nothing about. We want to offend no one, especially discussing a topic in which we have no formal training. I mean, what do we Hanson's know about art? Jeff is already, admittedly, the accidental artist—and a visually impaired one at that! It's hard to give a lot of credence to any opinions we might have about the art world. And we in no way want to imply that his paintings can compete with the artists or museums mentioned above.

But still, Jeff's art work has managed to successfully percolate its way to the surface of the art market, through our bumbling, backwards business. I feel I need to try and explain, to the best of my limited knowledge, just what has occurred. How did Jeff's uneducated, naive, unique valued product come to be accepted—not by art critics—but even better—BY PEOPLE WHO BUY ART!

And are they buying the art, or Jeff's story, or a little of each?

Here are Jeff's (and his parent's) observations on art—specifically, visual art (I just love that name. Perfect for the low vision artist).

The names, dates and places have been changed so I don't get sued.

I picked up a copy of the *Los Angeles Times* (that's right, not the *Kansas City Star*), and read about an "important new work" from an artist opening at a gallery in San Antonio (that's right, not Kansas City). The gallery had invited the artist to randomly select three words from the dictionary, and then create an important new work based on his inspiration, as the three words "spoke to him."

OK, I have a problem with this right away. *Important, new, work?*

I'm an ER doctor. I am struggling with the word "important" here. Using the word "work" is questionable. I'll go along with "new," for now.

A 60-year-old hospital employee, Dr. Jones (a radiologist, not a dermatologist), wandered into my ER one day, complaining of sudden dull pressure in his chest. He didn't want to check in as a patient. He just wanted to know if I thought the pain could be significant. He wanted an informal, curbside consult. He then proceeded to **drop dead**, mid-sentence, falling over onto a bed. DRT! Dead right there! (Yes, I did feel the chest pressure was probably significant).

It was time for me to do some *important, new work*. Dr. Jones needed some electricity. He had come to the right guy at the right time. I just happened to have a defibrillator.

"Charge!...Clear!...Zzzzzzzzzt!" A little twitching...and voilá...Dr. Jones could finish his sentence.

He later told me that he found my new work on him to be very important. Need I say more?

That's the definition of *important new work*.

So, back to the artist. He chose three words from the dictionary—*third, anger, response*. And then proceeded to bind multiple old cardboard boxes with rounds of plastic wrap, creating a giant glob that seemed ready for placement on a pallet and hoisting up on a shelf at Home Depot. But instead, it was mounted to the wall of the gallery, and drew thousands of viewers, seeking the deeper meaning of "Anger's Third Response." Gazing at the giant "installation," (love that word, like a new furnace or kitchen counter-tops), all I can say is, it changed me forever. It spoke to me. Yes, it most definitely was "Anger's Third Response." *The Visual Arts* section of the newspaper reviewed this important, new work, describing it as a "respectable installation" and "raw, but not overwhelming." Amen to that! I will never look at my Wednesday morning trash recycling the same way.

I handed Jeff the dictionary and helped him select three words. *Diethylene glycol, hairline* and *gag*. I suggested he go create an important new work. He stared at me for a moment, and went back to his iPad.

Another newspaper (nowhere near Kansas) reviewed the installation of another important work (ahhhh! those words again—Zzzzzzzzt. Zzzzzzzt!), this time inspiring us by leaning long, dead branches all around a huge old dead tree at a local arboretum. The viewer would be allowed to experience the evolution of the piece as it decayed, with weather, over time. The *artist* was mirroring the human experience. Yes, just what I was thinking. But I don't want to be reminded that I am weathering and decaying. Take a Prozac! Get happy! Zzzzzzzzzzzzzzzzzt!

This isn't a hard market to conquer, folks!

A trip to Chicago found Jeff staring at an installation (God, I love this...OK, I promise that's the last time I'll use that word) that looked like a Haitian earthquake victim's leanto shelter. But it had a certain *Star Wars* vibe to it, also. I could see why it warranted so much space in a prominent museum. It was art. It made me feel alive, human and in need of a droid or a wookie.

Remember, we are not art critics. These are just our observations on art.

So what is so unique about Jeff's valued art product? What does Jeff do that sets him apart? Why do people spend their hard-earned money on an untrained, low vision kid's paintings? Why am I not poking fun at his artistic creations?

It seems Jeff had some rules in his own mind, about what art should be, way back when he started painting note cards at age twelve. Guidelines to follow, so the results would be a "sight for sore eyes." As seen through **his** eyes. What was most pleasing to **him**. No one taught him these rules. And they were never discussed. No one, including Jeff, realized he was following any rules. Maybe they were a consequence of his low vision, subconsciously applied to his art, to compensate for what he couldn't see. Or maybe he was just born with a gift for color and design.

It has taken his mother and I the longest time to realize this. And until this writing, to even put it into words. When I overheard the patient in the doctor's waiting room say, "those paintings are by Jeff Hanson—I'd know his work anywhere," I was astounded. That meant Jeff had a certain look—a style. **I never noticed!** Which meant he had certain guidelines he would adhere to as he painted, causing a consistent, reproducible artistic product. A unique product.

And apparently the rules that Jeff accidentally, unintentionally follows, that define his style, happen to appeal to lots of main-stream art buyers. I say mainstream because Jeff's average customer is not shopping for expensive, high-end, intricate portraits. Jeff is not painting bowls of fruit here. No fine botanical ink drawings. No polo players on horses. The kid sees about 20/80, best corrected vision, through Swiss cheese. He is creating large, bright, bold splashes of color, with little detail, that happen to look great on a lot of people's walls.

So what are Jeff's "rules of art?" I asked him, and here is how he described these previously unwritten laws. This took some doing, as he never thinks about this—it's all at a subconscious level. (I imagine the same concepts have been written up in art texts, and taught in art schools everywhere for centuries—the same schools that brought you "Anger's Third Response." But Jeff hasn't attended art school, and offers these from his untrained, naive observations).

Jeff's Twelve Subconscious Rules of Great Accidental Art

1. SCALE Sitting in a large lounge on a cruise boat, we happened to glance across the room at the art work on the far wall. Twenty identically matted and framed-in-black pencil sketches, each about a foot square, hung together in a neat grouping. The framing alone was probably quite expensive, as were the sketches (*Pablo* somebody). But it was all wrong! There was no impact. No color. No pop. I couldn't even tell what it was, until I got very close to it. So you can imagine what the low vision kid thought of it. And it's a shame, because the art work was expensive and "critic approved." And you know an interior designer was paid a fee to "design" that space. (And I bet they had normal vision). But what a waste. It was totally a

non-entity, hanging on that wall. The only artsy thing about it was that the twenty identical black frames matched. They would have had the same impact without the sketches. Don't even bother to hang these! Send them back to the museum.

Jeff's solution? Make it bigger! Hang a few large canvases, with art brought up to scale. There is nothing more frustrating than driving down a freeway, trying to read a billboard with tiny fonts and pictures. This seems so obvious. Just make it bigger.

Explore this the next time you are in a large home or public space. Is the art work proportionally correct for the space? You don't need an art degree to figure this out.

2. COLOR Why is everyone so afraid of it? Every house in our neighborhood is painted a tone of tan or beige, inside and out. Walk down any busy street and find a sea of earth tone shirts, black jackets and denim jeans. Are we all so insecure? Must we all look the same? Jeff rarely paints with earth tones. They make him sad. And they probably don't pop in his visual field. He needs color—bright color. In big, bold patches. This might be driven by his low vision. Purple is his favorite. Jeff says, "The painting isn't done until the purple goes on."

3. CONTRAST Highly contrasting colors must be included in the work. This again may be a consequence of Jeff's low vision. Large, bold stripes of black or dark purple often sweep across Jeff's canvases. Tone on tone is hard to see, and you won't find it in Jeff's work.

Crazy thick modeling paste, wooden dowels and wires, large globs of paint and torn strips of woven canvas all create the heavy texture that catch Jeff's eye.

4. TEXTURE Jeff moved to this early on, in his transition from note cards to canvases. Incorporating modeling paste, sisal rope, wire, strips of torn canvas and just huge globs of acrylic paint into his work, add chunky texture and relief to the canvas. Light catching the texture, and the resultant shadows created, increase the visual pop and 3-D effect—all important in the low vision world. Texture makes the art much more interesting. Landscapes "grow right off the canvas." They are fun to look at, and TOUCH! Jeff scoffs at the notion that art is for the eyes only. He wants signs under his paintings that say "please touch the art!"

5. DEPTH The chunky texture is part of the depth. But the **canvas** also needs depth, so that it juts off the wall. Jeff only paints on 2.5" deep canvases, so they protrude a bit into the room. Then he paints the edges of the canvas, so the art work wraps itself around the sides. When you approach Jeff's art from the side, you are already catching a glimpse of the piece. His art is never framed, so the viewer can appreciate this 3-D effect.

6. AREA OF CALM Jeff is not fond of art work with "a million little busy things happening all over" the canvas. Areas of colors, then smeared and splattered, then dripped upon, then overwritten with a pencil, drawing tiny little meaningless sketches of nothing. It's very difficult to see, even with 20/20 vision. And try stepping back. The scale is all wrong. Tiny little marks have no business residing on a large canvas. Your eyes don't know where to go first. If the artist chooses to do that, keep it to one area only. Next to it, place an area of calm. A large patch of undisturbed, true color.

7. SUBJECT MATTER Jeff doesn't create any detailed art because of his limited vision and skill. He doesn't even like to try. Especially no people or animals. He prefers an abstract, contemporary style. Nothing concrete (or very crude concrete images, at best). His floral landscapes, which may appear detailed from a distance, are really composed of spooned-on globs of paint that mimic flowers. What appears to be detailed is actually quite crude. That's the best his vision allows. And buyers don't seem to care.

But Jeff's subject matter is often inspired by concrete things, such as panoramic views seen in travels. He often posts his inspiration for a painting adjacent to the completed work, and only then do you see what he sees. But it won't be a detailed bowl of fruit.

Jeff believes that finely detailed, realistic paintings have lost importance in our technological world. There was a time, before cameras, when artists needed to capture precise detail on canvas to record people and events. How else would we know how George Washington or Peter the Great looked? But with the advent of photography, and now the digital age, there is no need to create fine precise paintings of our world. Cameras do it so well, it becomes a wasted effort. The subject matter of a painting should be abstract, unreal, or presented in a new way. Something that captures the imagination. The intangible. Something you can't just go snap a picture of with your phone. The digital era will signal the end to bowls of fruit.

Inspired by travel. We take countless photos during family vacations, enabling Jeff to enlarge and review them on the computer once home. Showing Jeff the world while he still had some vision became a huge priority from 2005-2010. Never be caught without a coordinating umbrella during a brief shower on the island of Burano, off the shore of Venice. Burano Canal. M & M Candy Aisle, *in NYC looks good enough to eat. A poppy field in France inspired* Walk Through Provence.

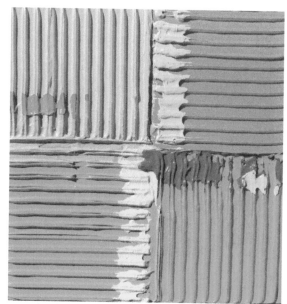

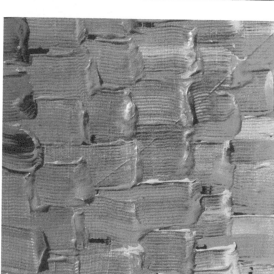

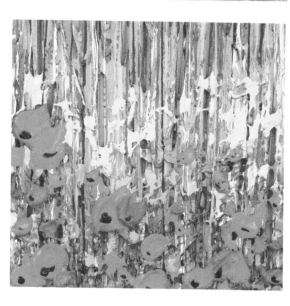

8. TITLE Every painting is given a title. And we have learned on many occasions that the title can sell the work. It might even be more important to the buyer than the art work itself. "Strolling Provence" will sell much faster than "Poppies in Bloom," especially if the buyer spent her twenty-fifth wedding anniversary in France. Naming art after places travelled is a great way to entice a buyer with added incentive. But never have the title specifically say what the painting subject matter is about. "Lunch in Pella" will sell faster than "Tulips in Pella." Jeff has retitled a "slow mover" on more than one occasion, followed by a quick sale.

9. DEFINITION/BLURRING It's easier to paint blurry lines when you have blurry vision. And part of Jeff's style is to blur or fade the transition between two colors or areas. He does this intentionally, so that things don't appear too "taped-off," or contrived. It also occurs because his canvases are so heavily textured that there aren't any sharp lines.

10. PAINTING IN LAYERS Jeff's most important technique. I always thought artists painted a canvas like I paint a wall in our living room. You start on one side and work across to the other. By the time you get across, you have a bowl of fruit. But Jeff has his own method. The canvas gets painted a background color, like my wall. But then, it is repainted multiple times in a variety of colors, using varying techniques, allowing the texture to create skips which permit the background to bleed through. There might be a dozen layers. In the end, he has created a very complex appearing work.

More travel inspiration. Window Box in Luss, *Scotland;* Krini Rooftop, *in Krini, Korfu, Greece; and* Jalousie Bay, *in St. Lucia.*

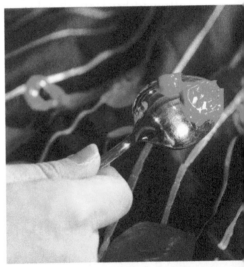

Tools of the trade. Jeff does use paint brushes to put down base coats. We all join in to cover each canvas with a color. But then the tools come out to create the patterns and texture that make the art work unique.

11. TOOLS Most of Jeff's painting tools come from Home Depot, not an art store. Putty knives, scrapers, tile trowels, rollers, Q-tips, spatulas and occasionally paint brushes are all used. Anything that creates more texture is a bonus. He paints sitting with the canvas on the floor. No easel. Jeff's acrylic paint is applied so heavily that it would ooze to the floor if the canvas stood vertically.

12. SIGNATURE Due to Jeff's low vision, his signature on a canvas is quite large. He signs on the 2.5" edge rather than on the conventional front lower right corner. But that in itself becomes another unique feature of the art. There is no doubt who the artist is, due to this "billboard" signature style. Flaunt your faults! So many artists sign in a tiny unrecognizable scribble. Jeff's large, proud signature boasts quality, value and clearly defines the piece as an *important, new work!*

With these rules of art revealed, you see that Jeff doesn't rely on great skills taught at an art institute. He simply, subconsciously, applies these techniques to his work, unknowingly creating the Jeff Hanson style. And he has had a great deal of success with it. Accidentally.

We are flattered by occasional comments that "there's no way a low vision kid could create that art! Someone else is painting for him." We are thrilled people think the paintings are that great! The combination of heavy texture and multiple layers do create a very complex result. But applied one step at a time, the process is easy for Jeff, despite his vision. (I'm not sure if it's the putty knives, the spatulas or the tile trowels that make it seem so impossible).

****

Being an accidental artist naturally led to the creation of some accidental art. Peculiar, serendipitous things can happen when you begin experimenting with paint squirted from bottles and random spills on your smock. Several times Jeff has realized that some of his splashes and "mistakes" are just as fun and marketable as the intended art.

For example, Jeff often aims jets of paint squirted from plastic bottles at a canvas—sometimes 50 or 100 different colors. But in addition to hitting the canvas, the flying paint also lands on pieces of cardboard protecting the basement floor. Or a backdrop of large canvases beyond the target, that just happen to get in the way. Or lands on my old doctor's lab coat Jeff wears to protect his clothing. These unintended creations of color sometimes turn out better than the art itself. Clients coming to our home to purchase art or watch Jeff paint often ask if "that piece of cardboard is for sale?" Or that "technicolor dreamcoat." We thought they were kidding at first, but soon realized there was a market for these as well. So Jeff started intentionally letting the paint fly even more, and now sells these accidental works (coined "The Studio Floor"), along with the intended ones.

But I had to step back and look at these *pieces of art* and ask if they were just Jeff's version of "Anger's Third Response." Was he really any different, after all? I mean, I was staring at a piece of cardboard with paint splattered on it. Were these just Jeff's *important new work?*

The answer, I believe, lies in the artist's intent. If the artist is trying to speak to their audience and convey a message, then the

Accidental art. The "grasses" were not intended to be the end product. They were simply standing to catch "flying paint" being squirted towards another canvas. But these backsplashes turned out better than the intended art, and were salvaged to decorate our guest room. Friend Kris dons a painted lab coat that she just purchased at a fundraiser. Jeff stands with a cardboard piece of the "studio floor."

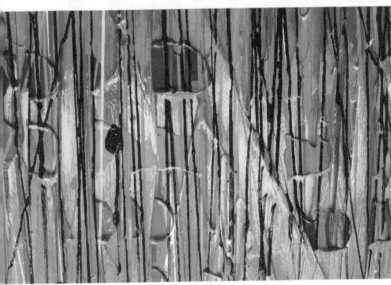

Looking through grasses. Jeff is unable to create detailed concrete images. He disguises distant objects by partially obscuring his view, as if looking through tall prairie grass. He gives the illusion of painting detailed things, but really only hints at them.

message shouldn't originate as random words from a dictionary or random drops of flying paint. That seems rather insulting, or deceiving. There should be some creative painting, with intent. But Jeff's art has no message. His art is intended to be a "sight for sore eyes," not change your life. He is just trying to decorate a room with happy, hot colors. Joy. There, that's the message. If it happens to be a piece of the studio floor, so be it.

Which leads to the question, "what is great art?" Jeff doesn't know. His parents don't know. Certainly not Jeff's...I don't think, anyway. He paints no bowls of fruit, has no talent or ability for fine detail, and no message.

But if you get the right person to say it is great, it could become great. Look around. There's a lot of strange stuff out there folks, hanging in very prestigious homes, galleries and museums. You call it great...and it becomes great! Just shout it loudly. You can create your own fame. Which seems weird and unfair, but we believe it is true. (So, we're going to start calling Jeff's art *great* and see what happens. Shhh! It will be our little secret).

Jeff had a fun encounter with billionaire Warren Buffett (it's true, keep reading), and gifted him a canvas. So now it's in the Buffett *collection*? How many artists out there can say this? Line up. But does that make Jeff's art great? Or does **where** it hangs make it great? (Who *collects* you, Jeff?) It's the same art that used to hang in our home in Kansas City. Was it great then, too? Creating fame.

Jeff Hanson's GREAT art does not currently hang in any galleries, and certainly in no museums. We all assumed Jeff needed that feather in his cap for clout and credibility, however. So we tried the gallery thing, and had very mixed feelings. True, the artist gets more exposure to a variety of art lovers. With wine and cheese, they browse the gallery for entertainment. But they usually aren't art **buyers**. "Here, let me just dust this painting off for you, and we'll have a look at it." And when they do buy, the gallery takes half. Now that might be OK if your art isn't selling any other way. But Jeff's appearance on stage at live charitable auctions has created a lot of exposure and sales. In fact, he has never caught up on commissions since 2008. His paintings are not gathering any dust. So giving half the money away seems like bad business. Especially since Jeff is trying to give a portion of his profits to charity.

People ask Jeff where they can find his art work.

"What gallery? Where is it hanging?"

Never wanting to be a name dropper, Jeff says "at my house."

Sounds prestigious, doesn't it?

Perfect marketing plan for a backwards business.

Those are Jeff's observations on art.

This chocolate on gold "drizzle" was intended to be totally abstract, and was painted as you see it. But as it leaned against a wall upside down, it took on a whole new meaning. What do you see? Jeff's one and only (thank God) bowl of fruit, 2009.

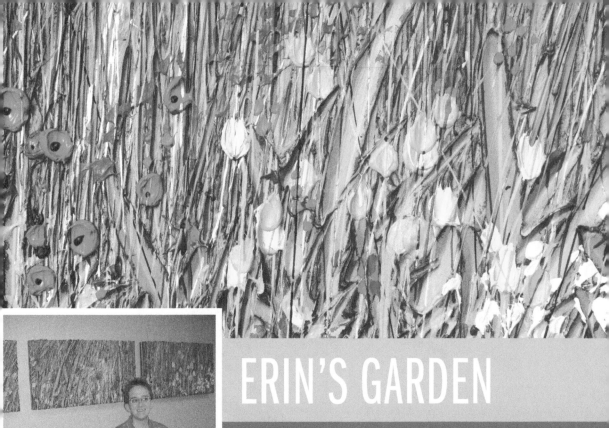

ERIN'S GARDEN

Painted in honor of Julie's wedding Matron of Honor, Erin Boylan, this five canvas work spanned 200 inches. It was gifted to Montgomery County Memorial Hospital in Red Oak, Iowa, in 2010, to decorate their new out-patient waiting area.

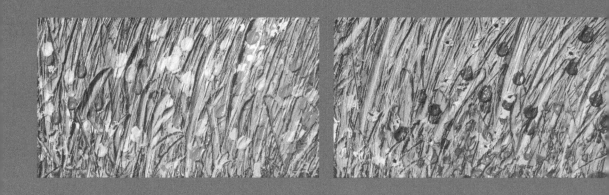

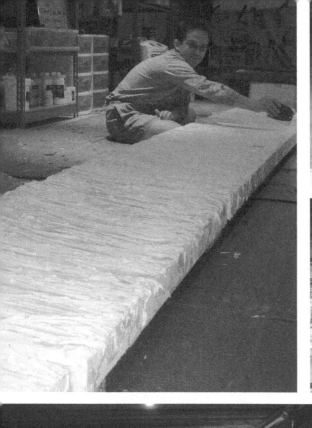

On Philanthropy

"It is far better to give than to receive."

Those were always hollow words for me. They sound nice to say, but in reality, I never really believed them. I simply could not internalize this. Why was it better to give? What's so great about it? I'm selfish. I like getting stuff. As a child opening Christmas gifts, the concept seemed downright insane! "Yes, I want an electric train, and no, I wouldn't enjoy giving you one instead! My train!!"

Growing up relatively poor, there wasn't much we could afford to give away, anyway. Charitable giving was for rich people. Rockefellers. Andrew Carnegie. People so rich they don't miss a million or two lying around. But I had no role models for charitable giving in my home. My parents didn't do this. And Julie's upbringing was similar.

Of course, we gave to our church, and neighbors in need. That is philanthropy, in a sense. But we didn't give to perfect strangers. Not to causes in faraway places.

Even as an adult, philanthropy was not a part of me. Not until my near-blinded 12-year-old son taught me about "giving" at a lemonade stand.

(phil an´ throp ist) One who loves humanity and works to promote human welfare. One who has the inclination to increase the well-being of human kind, as by service, charitable aid or donation.

Jeff's backwards business was founded on a philanthropy-first model. Not intentionally, but that is how it played out. And our entire family found joy in the process. More than joy—we caught the *philanthropy-first fever*! I really can't explain it. It wasn't planned, it just happened. In fact, we have become consumed by it. I can't imagine our daily lives without an emphasis on giving.

Jeff was thrilled to become **defined by generosity,** instead of CLOD. And his parents quickly hopped on the philanthropy bandwagon.

Jeff coined this tagline in 2008. "Every act of kindness helps create kinder communities, more compassionate nations, and a better world for all...even one painting at a time." And he lives by that.

I asked Jeff how it felt, at age 14, to hand Elton John a check for $1000. (Of his own hard-earned money). More specifically, would he do it again, if he could replay that night, backstage.

"Yes, I would definitely do it again. It was so much fun. I wanted to show Elton there was a whole side of me besides a poor Make-A-Wish kid losing his vision from an optic tumor. And it felt good knowing how many kids it would help through the Elton John AIDS Foundation."

"But think what you could have bought for yourself with $1000. That's a lot of money at age 14. Lot's of toys and gadgets."

He thought a moment. "Whatever I would have bought would

be long gone by now. I wouldn't even remember how I spent it. But the memories and good feeling last forever. I never would have got to know Elton. Not really. Dubai probably would not have happened. I'll never forget that. Elton would not have gifted The Children's Tumor Foundation. I wouldn't have sent art to the South African orphanage, or created note cards to support them."

"Generosity begets generosity?"

"Huh? Well I didn't realize all that would happen when I handed Elton the check, but it is really cool that it did, and I wouldn't trade it all for $1000."

"So you are a philanthropist."

"I guess so."

There is a dynamite little book called *The Go-Giver,* by Bob Burg and John David Mann, that specifically addresses the topic of "giving," and its effect on a business. Though written in 2007, we did not discover the book until 2011. A friend recommended it, as well as our strategic business planners.

The Go-Giver is not about businesses making cash gifts to charity. It is giving of yourself, your outstanding service and your passion for your product. It is about giving so much value, or perceived value in your product, service or idea that it becomes irresistible to the consumer. Giving your customer such an incredible experience with your product that they will have to share it with others, who will come beating down your door. *(Jeff's Bistro?)*

Jeff created that perceived value, and buying *experience* for his unique, valued product, by sharing his story and philanthropic spirit with his art customers. Sharing of himself. And then he took "giving" to a whole new level by donating most of his proceeds to charity.

Which added to his story, creating even more perceived value.

We read *The Go-Giver* and were astounded that the authors perfectly described what we had just lived through, for the past five years. Blindly, we had accomplished what they were preaching. Giving. We had no awareness, experience or other business reference point to compare to, but the authors' extensive business experience perfectly predicted our little backwards business' "stratospheric" success. We thought we had invented the wheel with our philanthropy-first model, only to learn that truly successful business people had been using this powerful idea for years. Giving. "All the great fortunes in the world have been created by men and women who had a greater passion for what they were giving—their product, service or idea—than for what they were getting" in financial return. The thing is, not many businesses are practicing this, and that is why there are lots of business failures and not so many Rockefellers.

The authors contend that businesses need to drop the profit-driven, "go-getter" attitude, and focus more on becoming "go-givers." And that your true self-worth in life is measured by how much more you gave than you received. *(It is far better to give...)*. Sounds crazy, but trust me, we have become believers! We need to talk to these guys. (I swear they must have dined at *Jeff's Bistro*).

Doesn't this sound a lot like Elton John telling Jeff, "If you give to the world, the world will give back?" And in the "Circle of Life," when he sings, "You should never take more than you give?" These ideas are not new. And not very complex. But very powerful in the business world, as well as in personal life. Giving.

Jeff had no intention of using his "go-giver" attitude and notoriety gained from charitable giving at *Jeff's Bistro* to drive his profitable art business. That would only raise concerns about insincerity and hypocrisy. He honestly, naively created his philanthropy-first business simply for the fun of it. He just wanted to give. But why? Why give? Why not be selfish? Why does anyone give anything to charity?

The answer is obvious in the corporate world. Most businesses promote corporate social responsibility (CSR) and philanthropic giving as ways to separate themselves from their competition. And there is commercial benefit to be gained by raising their reputation with the public and building customer loyalty. Strategic philanthropy. There is even an International Corporate Philanthropy Day on the fourth Monday each February, intended to build awareness of corporate-community partnerships and to inspire businesses around the world to engage further in corporate giving.

But what about individuals? Why do they donate their time, their skills or give their hard-earned bucks to perfect strangers? With no personal gain in mind? And many times anonymously? We have discovered five reasons.

Reasons for Philanthropy

1. SPIRITUALITY For starters, the answer is easy if you are a spiritual person, and can be found across many belief systems.

Those who are generous are blessed, for they share their bread with the poor. (Proverbs 22:9)

In all this I have given you an example that by such work we must support the weak, remembering the words of the Lord Jesus, for he himself said, "It is more blessed to give than to receive." (Acts 20:35)

The Torah recommends giving away ten percent of income to aid the poor.

You shall tithe all the yield of your seed, which comes forth from the field year by year. (Deuteronomy 14:22)

The Prophet Muhammad repeatedly emphasizes the importance of charity.

There is no person who does not have the obligation of (doing) charity every day that the sun rises.

But what about non-spiritual givers? Atheists. Agnostics. People who believe that when they die they will feel exactly as they did before they were born. People who live only for the present. And with death, their atoms simply return to that vast pool of universal matter, patiently waiting for their next molecular reassignment. What's in it for them? Certainly no rewards in the afterlife. Why do they give? Why not hoard it all for themselves?

2. GIVING BACK Most people, it seems, spiritual or not, *want to give back*. Looking back on their lives, people recall acts of kindness from others, gifts received, lucky breaks in life, unearned or unpredicted interventions or pivotal moments that changed everything. Like a black leather chair landing on your driveway. Or a trip to Dubai. People feel obligated to acknowledge and repay those debts. Rewarding random acts of kindness can be a great source of happiness for the giver.

3. LEGACY Or maybe they just want to make a difference on this planet. Leave their mark on society. A legacy. Give enough and society might even honor you with a statue.

4. EMPATHY Lots of philanthropists look around and see so much suffering that they show their empathy through charitable giving. After all, you can't take it with you. Andrew Carnegie. The Bill and Melinda Gates Foundation.

5. PURPOSE And most of all, charitable giving can give you **purpose**—a mission or calling. A day-to-day reason to keep going. Even if you have no other purpose for your existence, service to others and reducing human suffering can bring you great joy. Consider the AIDS orphans in South Africa.

Jeff's philanthropy was founded in all five of these reasons.

I came across an astounding quote with regards to having a **purpose** in life, and how you wish to be defined. In the Epistle Dedicatory to the play *Man and Superman*, the Irish playwright George Bernard Shaw (1856-1950) wrote:

"This is the true joy in life, the being used for a purpose recognized by yourself as a mighty one; the being thoroughly worn out before you are thrown on the scrap heap; the being a force of Nature instead of a feverish, selfish little **CLOD of ailments** and grievances complaining that the world will not devote itself to making you happy."

That was written in 1903. Be defined as a "force of Nature," not a "CLOD of ailments." George was speaking to Jeff.

It's not the challenge, but rather your response to the challenge that defines you.

Even our school system emphasizes the importance of "giving," community service and volunteerism. Students are expected to log 50 hours of community service each school year. I remember Jeff completing his requirement in the first month of each grade level. This was the one thing in school that was extremely easy for him. He nailed it. Slam dunk! While other students were struggling in May to come up with their meager, last minute, hours of service, Jeff was turning in record numbers—to the tune of 500 hours!

Philanthropic projects. The 604 hand-painted note cards were taped down all over our house, totally covering every horizontal surface. I had to eat standing up, holding my plate. Jeff gifted Kansas State School for the Blind Superintendent, Madeleine Burkindine, with some of his charitable proceeds, while a student there. Jeff is planning an encore for his 2009 Generous HeART calendar. Jeff was chosen for the Contemporary American Hero Award in 2011, from a neighboring school district. Fans Rob and Debbie Givens and his third grade teacher, Mrs. Miller attended.

Students would call Jeff and ask to come over and help paint canvases or note cards for charitable fundraisers, just to put in their time.

But for Jeff, this was how he found joy.

Jeff was performing community service in a number of creative ways. Of course, he painted lots of canvases and donated them to charitable auctions, which turned into dollars for the foundations in the end. By age 19, Jeff has done that more than 100 times (through 2012). And the printed note cards featuring his art are sold with all proceeds going to charity.

But Jeff also rings the Salvation Army Bells, volunteers at church and donates his artwork to other projects. In 2008, he hand-painted 604 cards with letters addressed to every optometrist and ophthalmologist in the State of Kansas, requesting donations to purchase new technology equipment for the Kansas State School for the Blind. "Project 604," he called it.

In 2009, Jeff created the "Generous HeART" calendar, with each month displaying one of his paintings, and honoring one of his favorite charities. Just something to do. He sold 7,500 of them locally and on-line. Proceeds from calendar sales were divided amongst the twelve represented foundations.

And then there are the gifts to children. Every year, Jeff creates multiple canvases of original art work for a children's facility, either local, national or international. His paintings hang in schools, orphanages, learning centers and hospitals. He laughs and says this is part of his Corporate Social Responsibility.

In the summer of 2009, we decided as a family to undertake our largest philanthropic effort to date. *The Generous HeART Show*. Giving. It was a fundraiser for our local Children's Hospital, and

The Elton John AIDS Foundation's orphanage in South Africa.

Jeff was emerging as an artist, as well as a philanthropist. It was time to do something big. *Jeff's Bistro* was just the warm-up. We all felt the desire to conduct a much larger philanthropic effort, and showcase Jeff's art skills at the same time. Create a little fame. For the first time, Jeff would be the sole-artist at his own show.

The idea was born when Jeff was approached by a local Kansas City businessman, Dan, who offered his office space as a venue for an art show. He had seen Jeff featured in the newspaper, and had coincidentally received some of Jeff's note cards as a gift. He was touched by Jeff's story, and wanted to join the philanthropic band wagon. For free. No strings attached. Giving.

The office space was in a magnificent, old, red brick building, fabulously restored into a high-tech contemporary business, smack-dab in the middle of the Kansas City Crossroads Arts District. And not only did Dan offer the venue, but he also provided live music, hors d'oeuvres and his Excel "A list" of business clients for the invitation list. 700 people. By invitation only.

The man's offer was so generous that Jeff decided there was no way he would receive profit from this art show. He decided to cover his costs, and then give the proceeds to charity. The Generous HeART Show.

So he painted. And painted. For four months, he painted. From March to July. Under Jeff's direction, Julie and I joined in the production of an astounding 135 canvases to be unveiled at the show.

July 23, 2009. We were ready. The venue looked spectacular. An estimated 500 people turned out, to meet the 15-year-old philanthropic artist with low vision, shake his hand, become part of his

Dan Nilsen, President of Kansas City business Bishop-McCann, generously offered his magnificently restored office space to host the Generous HeART show. Dan suspended metal panels from the high ceilings to display the 135 canvases. Killer space with killer art. An amazing event for the budding 15-year-old artist.

story and catch a glimpse of the world through his eyes.

The results—118 canvases sold in four hours! An overwhelming response. It was a buying frenzy! But did customers buy the art, or the story? Did Jeff's "Go-Giver" attitude make for this "stratospheric" success? Was the art that good, or the **place where it hung?** No matter the reason, everyone certainly was in the mood for giving.

Generosity begets generosity.

After covering his expenses, Jeff was able to gift our local Children's Mercy Hospital with $7,500 and Elton's Baphumelele orphanage in Khayelitsha, South Africa, with $6000 (a nice little entry for Jeff's community service log sheet). The Elton John AIDS Foundation was a regular recipient of Jeff's philanthropic gifts, ever since his Make-A-Wish was granted. In fact, EJAF's 2008 worldwide holiday greeting and solicitation letter highlighted Jeff's story and philanthropy.

Jeff was named global ambassador for the Make-A-Wish Foundation in 2010. He continued to fundraise for them, by donating canvases to auctions for several Make-A-Wish chapters around the country. Sometimes he would show up live, on stage in his tuxedo, to encourage the bidding. But he also came up with an idea to mass-produce his art for the organization (the budding entrepreneur?). Jeff developed a relationship with WHOLE FOODS MARKET, and he and Julie coordinated an agreement between Make-A-Wish and WHOLE FOODS to print Jeff's art work on reusable grocery bags at their stores in the Rocky Mountain region. Sales of the brightly colored bags generated $30,000 for Make-A-Wish of America.

Dollars to charity were continuing to climb. Jeff was interviewed by *CNN Headline News* in August of 2011, and was featured

October 2010, Orlando. Jeff posed with Allan Schmidt, founder of the Make-A-Wish
Foundation, as well as new "lit-up" Make-A-Wish friends from Connecticut.
In Dallas, local WFAA news anchor Shelly Slater helped Jeff
auction off a donated canvas for Make-A-Wish North Texas.

Jeffrey Owen Hanson LLC Dollars Generated for Charity

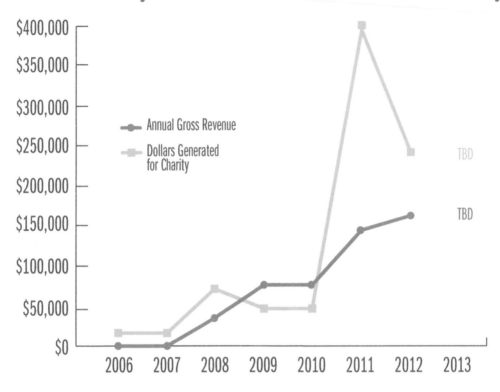

Legend:
- Annual Gross Revenue
- Dollars Generated for Charity

DREAM WISH BELIEVE

JEFF HANSON, AGE 17

As a former Make-A-Wish® kid, Jeff is helping paint a brighter picture by raising funds through his artwork.

Our Wish?

MAKING SURE THEIR WISHES COME TRUE.

When you donate to the Make-A-Wish Foundation®, you're helping fulfill the wishes of special children. In fact, 100 percent of the funds raised will be used to grant the wishes of children with life-threatening medical conditions. Ask your server how you can help. Because in order for them to wish big, they need a little magic from you.

Applebee's

For more information about the Foundation, visit wish.org.

ENRICH GIVE INSPIRE

Thank you!

Thank you for your donation to the Make-A-Wish Foundation®. With your help, we're able to make wishes come true for children with life-threatening medical conditions.

Applebee's

As Jeff's annual gross revenue trends upward, his dollars generated for charity have skyrocketed. The huge spike in 2011 is partly due to a collaboration with Applebee's restaurants. Jeff's artwork was featured on table stands and placemats in 247 Applebee's nationwide, encouraging patrons to donate to Make-A-Wish. Outstanding corporate social responsibility from a great company.

on "Leaders With Heart" and "Impact Your World." Jeff stated, at age 17, that his goal for the future was to "give a million dollars to charity." At the time, he had generated $350,000 for various foundations, and I smiled to myself thinking he could never attain his goal. But, one year later, Jeff's art work had generated over $750,000 for charity—more than doubled—and accelerating at a frantic pace! The one million dollar goal will probably be reached before age 20. Who else can say that? I can't believe I am typing this. Major deposit back into the "dream bank."

As the success of Jeff's art, philanthropy, and entrepreneurship unfolded, however, we tried as parents to step back and look at the big picture. Were we doing the right thing? This crazy-busy-art-philanthropy-business-thing? Should we allow this to continue? Was it time to shut down this whole snowballing machine? Was this even normal? (*Did any of us want to be **normal**?*) Becoming a celebrity? Creating fame? The philanthropic artist. Was that what Jeff wanted? Were we permitting Jeff to find time to "just be a kid?" And did he care?

He never expressed it, if he did.

Jeff was an only child. He lived in an adult world. Most of his friends were adults. Kids his age were living in a different world than he ever would. With normal vision. Driving a car. Attending a main-stream high school. Playing endless sports and attending endless social activities.

Jeff did not really have a peer group. Except adults. No kid was doing what he was doing. Nor did they really understand it. He had so little in common with kids his age that they almost had nothing to talk about. Jeff always needed to meet an art client, get a painting done by a deadline, or be in a tuxedo, on stage, promoting his art for a fundraiser. His peers weren't doing any of that. Likewise, Jeff knew nothing about soccer or basketball practice, skateboarding or biking. The two worlds never overlapped.

I found it somewhat sad to watch Jeff in a group of kids his age, because the interactions were cordial, but shallow, and uncomfortably polite. Not the silly, backslapping craziness that I recall from my high school. It made me uneasy to see Jeff in adolescent circles. He just didn't fit in. But I don't think Jeff ever noticed. He wasn't sad. He liked his adult world.

My uneasiness ended in May of 2011.

The Prudential Spirit of Community Awards represents the United States' largest youth recognition program based exclusively on volunteer community service. The awards were created in 1995 by Prudential Financial, Inc., in partnership with the National Association of Secondary School Principals to honor middle and high school students at the local, state and national level for outstanding service to others. The program's goal is to applaud young people who already are making a positive difference in their towns and neighborhoods, and even more importantly to inspire others to think about how they might contribute to the well-being of their communities.

Prudential has taken on the task of honoring kids throughout the U.S. who are champions of community service, philanthropy and volunteerism. It has become their Corporate Social Responsibility to spotlight teens for their social responsibility. (Who else is doing that?) At a corporate level, Prudential has made it a huge priority to search the United States each year, seeking out the 102 (two from each state, plus D.C.) most compassionate, community-minded,

WHOLE FOODS MARKET collaborated with Jeff and Make-A-Wish to sell reusable shopping bags designed by Jeff. Did you notice the purple? Tom Barnett, Jeff's lifelong mentor and swim instructor, helps celebrate the winning bid at a fundraiser. And Jeff turned the tables and became a "wish-granter" for wish kid and artist, Joanna, who wished for a day of art museums and shopping for art supplies with Jeff.

creatively philanthropic kids, and put them in the limelight, at an elaborate recognition ceremony in Washington, D.C.

Prudential's spotlight is not directed toward the high school football quarterbacks—not the All-State track stars—not the academic scholarship winners. They already got their trophies.

Prudential wants to showcase the kids with the longest, most creative, over-the-top list of community service hours logged in the nation. And they find them. Each year. In 2011, they screened 29,000 kids who were nominated for the Prudential Spirit of Community Award. The 102 state winners and their parents were invited to D.C. in May. And from those 102, only ten would ultimately be selected to win this national "Oscar" of community service.

In February, 2011, Jeff was informed that he was selected as one of the two Kansas winners for outstanding community service in our state. We were thrilled. Jeff's philanthropic spirit had again drawn national attention, and again defined him for his generosity. Jeff received a silver medal as a state winner and $1000 cash prize. And our family was invited to Washington, D.C. in May, for the announcement of the ten national award winners.

It was at the opening Prudential reception dinner for the 102 state winners, along with their parents, that my uneasiness about Jeff's peer group melted away.

Jeff was finally home. Far away from Kansas City. In Washington, D.C. Finally at home. Surrounded by people who spoke his lingo, and understood his passion. **This was** his peer group. These 101 kids that he had never met until that day. It was a room filled with people the most like Jeff he had ever met. Givers. From across America, screened and assembled by Prudential, they came together into one room. Everyone on the same page. Everyone shaking hands, immediately accepting one another and realizing they were not alone out there in their quest for philanthropy and community service. They were outliers—all of them—their achievements spilling way outside the bell curve for people their age. And they were all home. Finally surrounded by peers who understood them. Givers.

They didn't talk much about soccer scores or basketball, movies, clothes or cars. They each had a story to tell. A great story. Many even better than Jeff's story. They talked about "giving." They each had a project or passion that was changing the world. Many not just in their hometown, but at an international level. For Jeff, it was changing the world through art. But there were 101 other stories, equally as intriguing as Jeff's, of how each teen found a passion for a particular project, social concern or injustice. They too, were changing the world, each in their own way. 102 quirky, philanthropic kids, who didn't fit the usual teenage mold, who managed to find their way to this room on this day.

The chemistry and excitement were jaw-dropping!

And their parents. Julie and I talked to their parents for hours. Spectacular parents who had curiously watched their own child take this same peculiar path of philanthropy and community service at a very young age. We weren't alone after all. Parents sharing stories of stratospheric success in small family businesses, driven by young philanthropic hearts. Supportive parents, who went out of their way to foster a home environment that permitted 101 other *Jeff's Bistro's* to launch. Or to help their child get past their own CLODs, to find something **they can do**, to give back. (*Julie and I found our peers, too*).

And why did these kids give? Why was it better to give than to receive? There were 102 different reasons in that room.

After three days of sight-seeing, sharing, entertainment and dinners, all sponsored by Prudential, it was time for the national awards ceremony. The 102 teens and their parents had spent three days together, and we had learned many of the remarkable stories of philanthropy. We all had our favorites, of who might win the ten coveted awards. I had heard so many spectacular, compassionate, over-the-top stories by then that I didn't see how Jeff could win. All 102 were deserving, and it really didn't matter who took home the gold. I was excited for the awards, but dreaded the awards.

We assembled for a beautiful noon luncheon at the U.S. Chamber of Commerce, Hall of Flags. About 400 people in the audience. Excitement in the air. Live nationwide webcast. The 102 state winners going for one more medal.

Jeff had never shown much emotion about awards or recognition, but I could tell he really wanted to win this. It was a big deal. We had no idea what a big deal it was until we sat in that audience and watched. This was an extremely impressive assembly of young people, all marching to the beat of a different drummer.

One at a time, the ten national winners were called up to the stage, where they were introduced with a brief biography, and gold medal placed around their neck. They were each granted a $5000 gift from Prudential, as well as another $5000 to give to the charity of their choice. Extremely generous on the part of Prudential! Several of the winners we had met, and we cheered each one as if they were our own. After all, we were home. This was our family. Our peers.

I could see Jeff's disappointment, though, as each name was

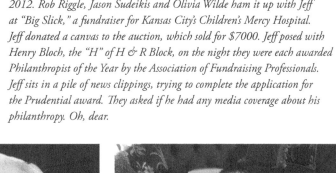

2012. Rob Riggle, Jason Sudeikis and Olivia Wilde ham it up with Jeff at "Big Slick," a fundraiser for Kansas City's Children's Mercy Hospital. Jeff donated a canvas to the auction, which sold for $7000. Jeff posed with Henry Bloch, the "H" of H & R Block, on the night they were each awarded Philanthropist of the Year by the Association of Fundraising Professionals. Jeff sits in a pile of news clippings, trying to complete the application for the Prudential award. They asked if he had any media coverage about his philanthropy. Oh, dear.

called up. He so wanted this, more than he had ever let on. He was 17. He had unknowingly been working toward this moment for five years, never seeking recognition, only giving because he wanted to give. He knew it was a huge, difficult thing to win. The competition was steep. The 102 most philanthropic teens in the United States. He had met them all and heard their stories. The cream of community service.

And then the eighth name was called.

"From Horizon Academy, in Roeland Park, Kansas, Jeffrey Hanson."

All three of us jumped to our feet and hugged. Jeff had a lot of new fans in the audience who cheered. Jeff was electrified. You would have thought it was the Academy Awards.

I whispered in Jeff's ear. "Every act of kindness helps create kinder communities, more compassionate nations and a better world for all…even one painting at a time."

Jeff stormed the stage for his award. As he stood at the podium and gazed into the audience, I knew he could not see us. But he could have heard our hearts pounding.

"For courageously turning his own health crisis into an opportunity to serve others, for using his talents to generate an astounding amount of money for important charitable causes, and for being an outstanding role model, we are proud to name Jeffrey Owen Hanson as a 2011 Prudential Spirit of Community National Honoree."

The words were not hollow anymore.

It is far better to give than to receive.

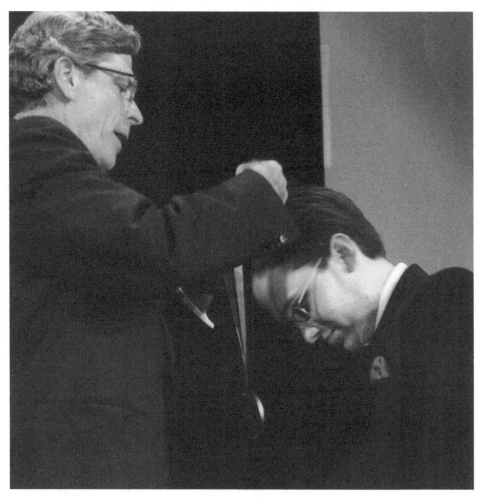

"From Horizon Academy, in Roeland Park, Kansas, Jeffrey Hanson." John Strangfeld, CEO and President of Prudential Financial, placed the "Olympic Gold Medal" around Jeff's neck. Better and more meaningful now, than the Olympic gold medal in gymnastics that was in my original dream bank. Jeff and National Prudential winner Rocco Fiorentino pose outside the capitol building on a tour of D.C. Rocco, a middle-schooler, is totally blind and has testified before congress to increase funding for Braille education in schools nationwide. Google his name and get ready for goose bumps, tears and smiles!

TRIP OF A LIFETIME

This heavily textured canvas was created in 2010 as a gift to the national Make-A-Wish Foundation in Phoenix, to decorate their corporate headquarters. Painted totally in "Jeff's colors," the canvas salutes the countless trips and wishes Make-A-Wish has granted to children in need, fulfilling their lifetime dreams.

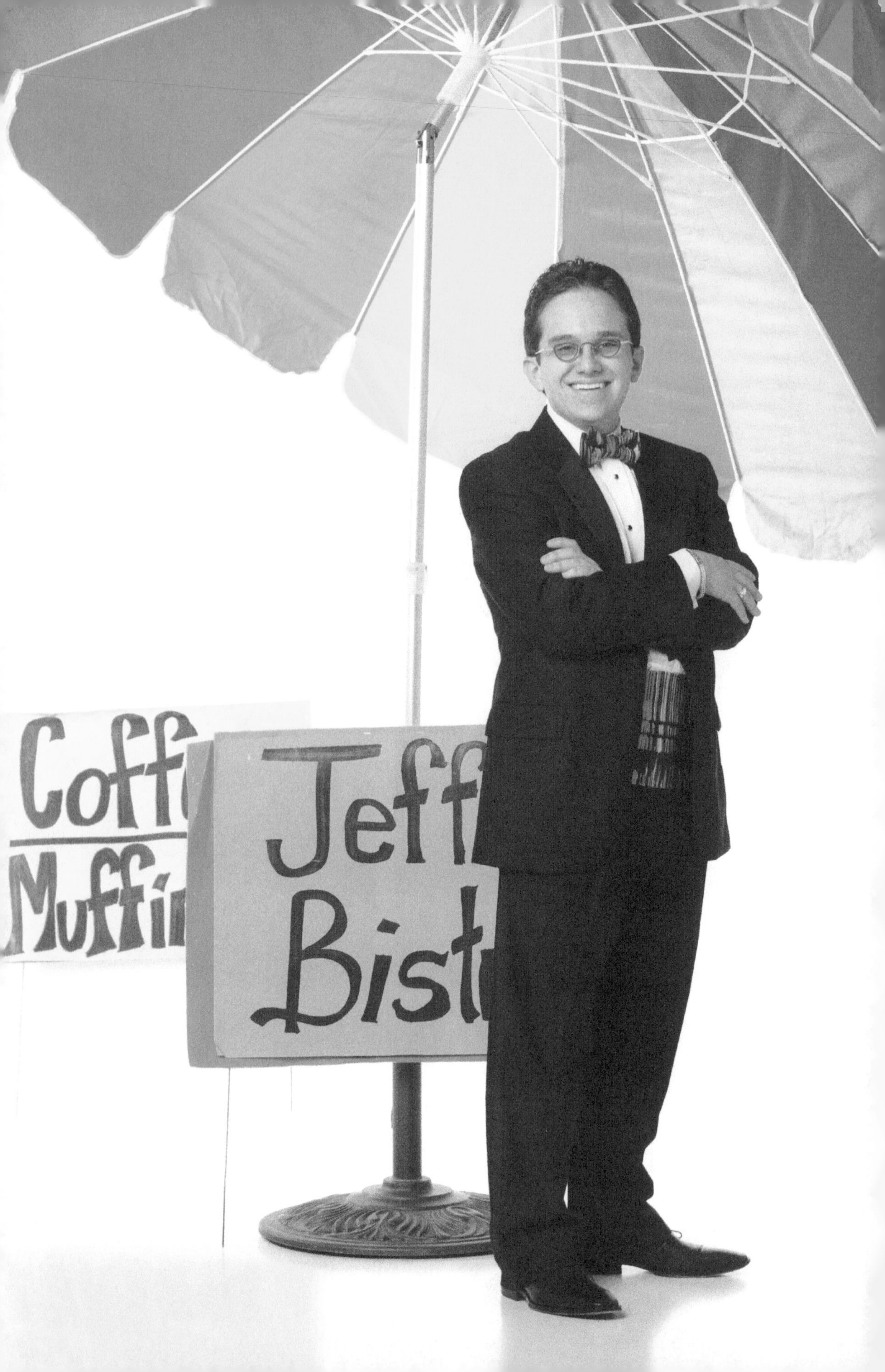
Coff
Muffi
Jeff
Bist

on Entrepreneurship

Jeff Hanson is an entrepreneur. He is the CEO of his own business. His mother is on the payroll as business manager, marketer, purchasing agent, social media consultant and painter's assistant. His father is his unpaid accountant, photographer, chauffeur, varnisher and gopher, hoping to be employed by him soon. The business, Jeffrey Owen Hanson LLC, is quite successful by The U.S. Small Business Administration standards, especially considering its humble beginnings.

The odds of starting and maintaining a viable new business, without experience in the business world, are slim. Fifty percent of new business upstarts in the United States close for various reasons over their first five years. Jeff has just successfully crossed that milestone. Statistics from the SBA would have predicted his doom in the first year or two. (But, of course, your business can't really fail if you don't know you have one).

So what makes an entrepreneur successful? Who are these people? The survivors? What characteristics define them? Are there any common threads? What will make one new business explode with popularity, while many others implode into bankruptcy?

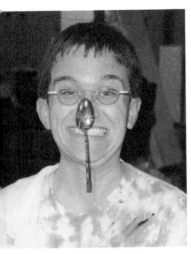  

The players. Jeff, the serious artist. Julie, (her cell phone cover has Jeff's art on it) in her lavish basement-corner office, and Hal, the author, painter's assistant and gopher. Theodore Edward "Wundy" Bear, family mascot and Jeff's older brother. The basement in chaos, as usual. I had dreams of a man-cave down there, The Egyptian Lounge and Tut's Bar. Forever erased from my personal dream bank. Our formal living room (never sat in there) became Jeff's home gallery.

(en tre pre neur´) one who organizes, manages, and assumes the risks of a business or enterprise. An innovator with a high need for achievement, who builds capital through risk and initiative, searches for change, responds to it, and exploits opportunities to launch a new venture.

Search the internet and you will find endless pearls and rules for small business success. Many concepts are deemed so important they appear on virtually everybody's list. "Have some experience in the field before starting your own business (*Oops!*). Secure enough capital for start up (*say what?*). Have a detailed business plan (*three years later?*). Know your competition (*nope*)."

Jeffrey Owen Hanson LLC probably isn't the best business to consult about reasons for success, given Jeff's backwards approach to the business world. But as a family, wallowing through a jungle of small business pitfalls, we can examine ourselves and make a few personal observations on entrepreneurship. Observations and ideas that got Jeff where he is today.

Jeff's list of "keys to success" might surprise you. None of them are on the SBA's list of successful behaviors. But they are paramount to Jeff. Some elements are so basic, you may not deem them worthy of consideration. But **do** consider them. Jeff doesn't talk about "finding your niche," or "planning for success." "Building a team" or "soft sell/hard sell" (he said this sounds like a menu at a taco stand). Jeff's pearls are straight out of *Jeff's Bistro*. Ideas he was using long before he knew he had a business. Ideas his grandmother taught him. Ideas that worked.

Jeff Hanson's Eight Entrepreneurial Pearls

1. STORY. It's everything! It's the number one reason Jeffrey Owen Hanson LLC exists. Unless you are planning to unleash a new "must-have" product as earth-changing and ubiquitous as the iPhone or GOOGLE, Diet Coke or the Model A Ford, you simply have to come up with a story. From CLOD, to *Jeff's Bistro*, to Elton John in Dubai, to art auctions and huge dollars to philanthropy, to community service awards—your business or product MUST have a story to draw attention.

But you don't need a brain tumor to spotlight your business. There are lots of creative ways to build a story around your product and promote it. Look at Tom's Shoes, for example. Their "One for One" program promises to give a new pair of shoes to a child in need, for every pair sold. Their website boasts over one million pairs of shoes given away as of 2010! That is incredible! It really gets my attention. And it makes me want to buy a pair of Tom's Shoes! They must be a great company! I want to do business with them! They have a great STORY! Did they have a brain tumor? No. Is their product earth-changing? It's shoes! They didn't really have a story at all. But they CREATED a great story. In their case, a philanthropic one.

The story can be anything. Look at your product and your business. Why do you exist? Where did you come from? What made you launch this company? Why do you have a passion for this particular product or idea? What problem needed to be solved? Tell your story. Is it a family business? Is there a skeleton in the family closet? Someone eccentric? Is there a secret family recipe? Is it all the recipes from your family combined into a Southern Cookbook? Tell me about your relatives. Especially the strange ones. Whose recipes are these?

Look at Bush's beans. They have created a STORY with Jay Bush's backyard barbecue media campaign, teaching us that the family dog, Duke, is secretly trying to sell the family bean recipe. It's a funny STORY. Eating their beans looks like so much fun. (And their family appears to get along at reunions). I want some of "them grillin' beans!"

What "brand" are the wooden toothpicks in your cupboard right now? Do they even have a brand? Somebody makes them. I want to know their story. Or I might start making my own "Hanson-picks," and create a story to grab a piece of the toothpick market. I believe I could create a "brand" of toothpicks with the right story, and establish name recognition.

Check out Annette Simmons' book, *The Story Factor*. It is an outstanding argument for the use of "story" as an effective tool to inspire, influence and persuade others. For new businesses, telling your purpose with "who am I" and "why am I here" stories will quickly influence customers to trust your new brand or product.

I talk like I always knew this. But I had no idea how effective STORY could be in promoting a business, until I witnessed Jeff unknowingly use it to perfection.

2. PHILANTHROPY. Or call it Corporate Social Responsibility. Or "Cause" Marketing. Or Strategic Philanthropy. Or Community Service. Or "Giving." For Jeff, philanthropy became deeply imbedded into his STORY, as it should be for every new business. Jeff's artwork has generated over $750,000 for charity, and he intends to top one

million dollars by age 20! (Jeff's new campaign: $1M20!). But his art business is also for profit. The philanthropy component drives his marketing and sales of commissioned works.

Every entrepreneurial venture needs to associate itself with a "cause." And make it well known. Flaunt it! Pick a social concern or foundation that aligns with your idea or product, and develop a relationship. It needn't mean a big financial outlay. It doesn't have to be money at all. It can be volunteer work to clean up a city park, or start a 5K Run to raise money for a charity. Whatever you choose, you must sincerely be passionate for the cause, and devote real time to it. Your customers will respond positively to your philanthropy. Generosity begets generosity.

A local bank recently sponsored a community drive to recycle old used electronics. Computers, old TV's, VCR's, etc. Simple flyers and signage advertised the one-day, drop-off event.

People came out of the woodwork. The bank parking lot was inundated. It was a huge success. Does recycling have anything to do with banking? Did the project cost the bank a lot of money? No, but cleaning up everybody's basement and garage struck a chord. And recycling environmental hazards is always a great "cause." And now a lot more people know where that bank is located, and how easy it is to get in and out. Great community service project demonstrating corporate social responsibility. It added to their STORY, too. I really feel good about that bank.

3. DRIVE. Set your alarm clock. Get up! Get going! Time's a-wasting! *Jeff's Bistro* umbrella always went up at 7 am. That meant preparation started at 5:30 am. Jeff was 12 years old then. (His parents were

a few years older). If you are really planning to start your own business, you need to look at yourself closely and see if you are cut out for this. Are you wired this way? Energetic? Tenacious?

Remember the Munchkin's lyrics from "The Wizard of Oz?" (Sorry, we're from Kansas). "We get up at twelve and start to work at one...take an hour for lunch and then at two we're done...jolly good fun!" This won't cut it in the entrepreneurial world. If you like to sleep till noon, play video games and watch TV all evening, that doesn't leave much time to develop your business. There is nothing wrong with that lifestyle. In fact, you probably will live longer than us type-A's. But you might be a much better **employee** of an entrepreneur, than the CEO. You need to be **driven** to develop and sell your product. You need to have so much enthusiasm for your unique, valued product that sleep and leisure become a nuisance. You must be willing to accept delayed gratification for your hard work.

Thomas Edison, the great American inventor and entrepreneur said, "Genius is 1% inspiration and 99% perspiration." Work up a sweat! Get going!

I have read several surveys about the sleep requirements of historical figures, celebrities, CEO's and high profile business people. (Leonardo da Vinci—15 minutes every 4 hours; Napoleon Bonaparte—4 hours; Thomas Edison—4 hours; Michelangelo—4 hours; and so on). There is wide variability, but many entrepreneurs report sleep patterns of 4 hours a night, with a 30-60 minute power nap in the afternoon. That seems a little extreme. And it might lead to decreased productivity in the long run. But it is commonly described. Jeff and his parents sleep 6-7 hours (11 pm to 6 am). But the point is, you can't sleep 12 hours and still find enough time to develop a new business. Most entrepreneurs report that "there are not enough hours in the day," and sacrifice sleep time for business development. If that won't work for you, consider being an employee of a budding business instead of the owner.

What about the topic of age and career development? Jeff started *Jeff's Bistro* when he was 12. Now that's a little extreme. But take a look at the world's superstars. Did they make it big when they were 50 or 60 years old? Steve Jobs. Miley Cyrus. Madonna. Warren Buffett. Lady Gaga. Elton John. Bill Gates. Justin Bieber. Name any movie star or music celebrity. Any current wealthy entrepreneur of the digital age. Most of them made it big when they were in their late teens or early 20's. They figured it out at a very young age. They were in a race for success. And they weren't sleeping till noon. They weren't playing sports every day. They were up early, taking care of business.

Steve Jobs said, "It is rare that you see an artist in his 30's or 40's able to really contribute something amazing." You don't need gray hair to become rich and famous. Look around. Who's producing? Who's got the creative juices flowing? Who's winning? Don't wait for fame. It won't come. You need to get off your duff and just go do it, now! Set your trajectory. The younger and sooner the better. Get up! Get going! Show some **DRIVE!**

Sports. It's ok to play sports. But…"everything in moderation." Sports are great for exercise, for physical and mental health, for learning teamwork, perseverance, for making friends. But every day? At the expense of everything else? An all-consuming obsession? To what end? To be one in a thousand that becomes a professional athlete as a career? If you really are that talented, by all means do it!

Chase your dream. But for the rest of us, rethink how you want to manage your time.

Participation in sports can be great. But don't **only** do that. Find something else. Find your niche. Find your passion, your career dreams. Don't do what everybody else does. Not every day. Reclaim a little time for yourself. Be creative. Do things **you** decide to do. Not things someone else **organized** for you to do, to fill your day. We have limited time here—don't waste it living someone else's life. If sports and organized leisure activities (including TV) are your only pastime, you are wasting your own creativity and entrepreneurial growth years.

4. UNIQUE, VALUED PRODUCT. I discussed this in Building a Business Backwards, but I'll say it again. You must have a unique, valued product. Unique is not enough. Your product must have perceived value as well, to get the public's attention and stand out amongst your competitors. I'm not talking about "dollars" of value. It's the STORY, the reputation of the product or brand, and the *experience* the customer has with it that creates the value, and makes your product sustainable.

Jeff's paintings are unique. That's easy. Each one is a unique original piece of art. And he doesn't copy anyone. But the value part, that comes a little harder. How does a no-name kid compete with the long-established art world, and suggest high prices for his art? It's all about the STORY, the PHILANTHROPY and the experience the customer has purchasing the art. It creates demand. "I want a piece of **that kid's** art!"

I believe my "Hanson-pix" (catchy, huh?) will be a unique,

valued product. Toothpicks are not unique. They all look the same. But toothpicks flavored like S'mores, that remind you of campouts as a child, are unique. And valued. *I can't use just any toothpick, it has to be a Hanson-pix.* Is this any different than people whose cell phone **has** to be an iPhone?

5. DREAM. Dream big! Never lower your sights. Shoot for the sky! No ambition is too huge, no dream too impossible. Never underestimate yourself or your business. Jeff Hanson started promoting his "kid art" in the big, cold, scary art world, alongside the most famous and greatest. Intimidating? Yes. But never stop dreaming. Remember, it is GREAT ART! Dream.

All great inventions, innovations and achievements started with a vision. Every cock-eyed idea—man can fly—man can walk on the moon—a kid can raise a million dollars for charity—started in someone's dream bank. Focusing on your dream for your business will make it happen.

Again quoting Steve Jobs, "Start small, think big!" "We're gambling on our vision, and we would rather do that than make 'me too' products. Let some other companies do that. For us, it's always the next DREAM."

The authors of *The Go-Giver* said, "What you focus on is what you get." "Being broke and being rich are both **decisions**." (Be careful what you wish for).

Can this be? Can you wish yourself a successful business? Can you dream it into reality? You bet! It's the only way. The power of positive thinking. The alternative is settling for less, or failure. DREAM BIG!

6. UNCONDITIONAL POSITIVE REGARD (U.P.R.) Don't go anywhere or talk to anyone without this life skill.

Read these questions out loud, and compare them.

"Do you need something?" vs. "How can I help you?"

"Where are you going?" vs. "Can I give you directions?"

"Do you work?" vs. "Who's your employer?"

Can you hear the difference? The first question of each pair has a little "stinger" of attitude attached to it. Subtle, but intimidating. "I'm the authority and you are not. I am superior to you."

It's not what you say, but how you say it, that has a big impact in your interpersonal relations. If you are trying to get someone to trust you, take your advice or buy your product, then offending them at the outset will be very counter-productive to your goal. Your attitude just got in the way. You must communicate in a manner that helps sell your unique, valued product. And how do you do that? Simple. Turn on your **U.P.R.**

Psychologist Carl Rogers (1902-1987) coined the term "Unconditional Positive Regard" to describe an attitude and approach that therapists should use toward their clients. It is a blanket acceptance and support of a person, regardless of what they say or do. Which means that if you disagree with a person's behavior, lifestyle, appearance, habits, language, dress, etc., you must look past that and treat the person with the same regard that you do your best friend. Unconditional positive regard. You must honor people, listen to them with an open attitude, suspend all judgment about them, and try your best to show that you are a caring human being who wants to help or serve.

Jeff and his parents feel U.P.R. is extremely important when interacting with coworkers, other businesses, clients and customers. From *Jeff's Bistro* to art auctions. So important, that it made Jeff's list of "top eight pearls." It is the basic "do unto others" attitude. The Golden Rule. And U.P.R. extends far outside our businesses, to our spouses, children, neighbors, (and yes, even our in-laws). By applying our attitude of unconditional positive regard, we learn to drop those offensive "stingers," and move on to more productive communication and sales. U.P.R. is a life skill that will bring far more happiness and success than shooting stingers. Smother them with kindness. It's great for business.

7. DIVERSIFY/FLEXIBILITY. You might start out your new business with a single product. You need to be passionate about it and develop it until you get it right. Start small, but think big. And keep looking ahead. Your business needs to grow and become sustainable. What related ideas, services or products can be developed to expand your business and bolster sales? What innovation will broaden your potential target audience? Don't be so rigid about your product, how you display it, market it or get paid for it. Let it evolve. Be flexible.

Listen to your customers. They will often tell you which direction to go. Jeff has many times moved into a new product because of suggestions from clients. Abstract paintings became Jeff's vague landscapes. Jeff had an orthodontist commission two large paintings with metal wires spanning across the canvases, to mimic orthodontic braces. Sound strange? We thought so too, until we helped Jeff create them. They turned out awesome, and have been requested by other customers since. Jeff listened to his customer.

Listen to your customers for ideas. Jeff created the signage for "Celsius Tannery," based on their logo and color scheme. Building Bridges *was a mixed-media work commissioned by a church and featured wires, a suspension bridge and nails to match their fundraising campaign theme. The "wires" idea originated with an orthodontist's request for metal.* Kapalua Sunset *spanned three staggered canvases, adding a whole new element to the art.*

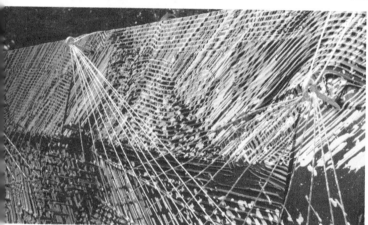

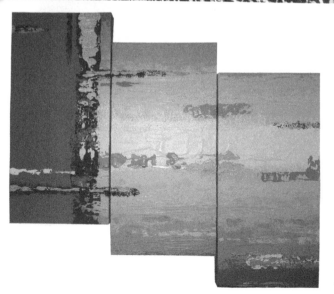

Diversify your products. Jeff has applied his art to note pads, chocolates, coffee and calendars. Jeff swapped artwork with businessman Leon Butler, for cool THEO eye glasses frames.

In the beginning, Jeff only painted note cards. He was asked by his eye doctor to transfer his note card art onto a canvas for a charity auction. That was a big step for Jeff, but look what happened.

Then came printed note cards, note pads and calendars. On the horizon, fabrics, fashion, and rugs. Motivational presentations. This book. It's endless. Always keep looking ahead. DIVERSIFY. Keep ahead of the competition, the copy-cats and trends. Don't follow the trends. Set them!

Jeff has even used diversification and flexibility in how he accepts payment for his art work. Several times he has bartered with clients or other businesses for their products and services. Jeff paid for his original web site with half cash, and half artwork.

Jeff loves designer eye glasses. He needs magnifying lenses to aid his low vision, so he figures he might as well wear something artsy and unique. A different pair for every outfit. (Could be the Elton John influence). There is one particular brand he is quite fond of, THEO. Made in Belgium. They come in hip, screaming colors and styles. But they are pricey.

Jeff negotiated with our local optical shop to swap art for eyewear. Jeff created very cool "glasses-themed" art for two of their stores, in return for his pick of THEO eye glasses frames.

Two great things came out of that negotiation. Optical shop customers saw the paintings, and inquired about the artist. Jeff's bold signature on the edge of the canvases, displayed in a public place, drew lots of attention. The art was a billboard advertising Jeff's art business. That led to more art commissions.

But the THEO sales rep visiting the optical shop also saw the art and heard the STORY of the artist and his bartering for THEO frames. She notified THEO headquarters in Belgium about the philanthropic artist trading art for their product.

What did THEO do? They commissioned Jeff to create five large original canvases, in hot THEO colors, to be displayed at the SILMO Paris International Eyewear Exhibition to decorate the THEO booth. The "O" themed canvases were titled *Crazy 'Bout THE-O*. Jeff's first international commission. All because Jeff was flexible and creative with the sale of his art, and his reimbursement.

8. THE POWER OF THE HAND-WRITTEN NOTE. Our world has gone digital. And our correspondence so very impersonal. Texting. Email. Facebook. Twitter. Schools have stopped teaching cursive writing, in favor of keyboarding. The postal system is going bankrupt.

Here lies an opportunity to stand out in a crowd. To revitalize a lost art. To be noticed.

How many hand-written letters do you receive each week? One? None? I guarantee, the younger you are, the fewer you have received. But isn't it fun, and refreshing to open a hand-written letter? Like it might contain something that you actually want to read? *The writer spent a lot of time, and sincerely cared enough to write me personally.* WOW! Think how you can use that in your business.

It was Julie, Jeff's mom, who insisted that Jeff write a hand-written note to every aunt, uncle and grandma who ever sent him birthday money. To every customer who purchased a canvas from him. To every business he collaborated with on a project. To every charity that had him on a live auction. "It's just proper etiquette," she says.

And time and time again, people have responded back, impressed and astounded that Jeff bothered to take the time to write a short note, personally. Despite his low vision and trouble with penmanship, Jeff sends original, hand-painted, hand-written cards. It really gets their attention. And it is an absolutely fool-proof tactic for a new business (or any business), to make your product or service become even more unique and valued.

I know what you are thinking. You are thinking that this can't be that important. That an email will do just as well. Our observation is, however, that this is an extremely powerful and underutilized tool that can have a huge impact. A very simple, concrete suggestion, to make your entrepreneurial endeavor stand out above the crowd. Try it. The power of the hand-written note.

In a nutshell:

Story. The number one thing a new business needs.

Philanthropy. Makes a great addition to your story. Find a "cause."

Drive. Get up. Get going. Just do it!

Unique, Valued Product. With "story and the *experience*."

Dream. If it's good enough for Steve Jobs…

Unconditional Positive Regard (U.P.R.). In everything you say and do.

Diversify/Flexibility. Let your unique, valued product spread its wings.

The Power of the Hand-written note. Because Warren said so.

****

Warren Buffett is widely considered to be the most successful investor of the 20th century. Consistently ranked among the world's top five wealthiest people, he is the chairman, CEO and primary shareholder of Berkshire Hathaway. In 2012, at age 81, *Time* magazine considered him one of the most influential people in the world. The "Oracle of Omaha." Mr. Buffett is also a notable philanthropist, pledging to give away 99 percent of his ($50 billion plus) fortune to charity.

The history of Berkshire Hathaway is storybook. In 1979, BRK began the year trading at $775 per share, and by year's end at $1310. When BRK began selling their class "A" shares in 1990, the market closed at $7,175 per share. Historical high for the stock was a whopping $150,000 a share (never had a stock split) in December 2007. A fairly sound investment for those who listened to Warren from the beginning.

We have friends living near Omaha, who got into Berkshire Hathaway on the ground floor. They aren't working any longer.

How did Warren Buffett achieve this? Starting out as just your average kid? Growing up in Omaha and Washington, D.C.?

The guy is a "natural-born entrepreneur." With incredible DRIVE, energy and creativity. There are numerous anecdotes about his early years, and the business ventures that got him started. Warren filed his first income tax return at age 14, deducting the cost of his bicycle and wrist watch used on his paper route. At age 15, he bought a used pinball machine and placed it in a barber shop. He soon had multiple machines in multiple barber shops. He sold stamps, and golf balls, and detailed cars. And so on. Nothing very complicated. But lots of ambition. Ceaseless energy. Always on the lookout. Perceiving an opportunity, he would position himself to take advantage of it.

Jeff loves this kind of STORY. Over-the-top success, incomprehensible riches and selfless PHILANTHROPY. And in 2008, when the opportunity presented itself for Jeff to start a Roth IRA, he naturally "wanted in" on Warren Buffett's track record and gold mine. After some research, Jeff purchased one of Berkshire Hathaway's "B" shares as an investment.

But Jeff didn't stop there. Always DREAMING, always going straight to the top, Jeff decided to write a note to Mr. Buffett, just to let him know that he appreciated Warren's leadership as the manager of his investment. A **hand-written letter** on one of Jeff's note cards. He told Warren about his painting business, his philanthropic ventures, and encouraged him to visit his website and tell "his people" about it.

It took some time and patience to get Jeff's letter into Warren's hands. The CEO of Helzberg Diamonds (a Berkshire Hathaway company), Beryl Raff, who is also a Make-A-Wish national board member and fan of Jeff's, made it happen.

So what did Warren do? With this **hand-written** note, from a 15-year-old businessman? He wrote Jeff back. Himself. **Hand-written.** At age 80. The richest man in the world. He didn't need to do this. He has people. He's a busy man. But he wrote Jeff personally, acknowledging his letter, encouraging him, and inviting Jeff to attend the annual Berkshire Hathaway shareholder's meeting in May, 2010, as HIS GUEST. He said he would "have a special seat" for him.

We had no idea what this was. But we figured if Warren Buffett invited us, we should go. We had heard the BRK shareholder's meeting in Omaha was a big deal. In fact, along with the College World Series, it's one of the biggest annual events hosted by Omaha.

Dear Mr. Buffett,

My name is Jeff Hanson. I'm a 15yr old visually impaired artist from Overland Park, Kansas.

My commission canvas business allows me to invest for my future. Last week I bought my first Berkshire Hathaway B. My goal is to have an A share in a few years!!

I am planning for my future, however I also know the joy in giving to others. My goal is to raise $120,000 on my calendar and note cards, allowing me to gift $10,000 to each foundation featured in my 2009 Generous HeART calendar

Please share my story with your people and encourage them to visit my web site @ WWW. jeffrey owen Hanson . com.

I look forward to meeting you at the next annual meeting. Until then, buy low... sell high!!

your friend,
Jeffrey Owen Hanson

NOT A RECENT LIKENESS*

2-18-10

Hi Jeffrey,
Be sure to you to the annual meeting this year. Let me know if you can make it + we will have a special seat for you. your friend,
Wm E Buffett

*FOR OBVIOUS REASONS

Even Warren Buffett recognizes the power of the hand-written note. "Hi Jeffrey. Be sure to come to the annual meeting this year. Let me know if you can make it and we will have **a special seat for you.** Your friend, Warren Buffett."

As many as 27,000 shareholders attend. It's like a rock concert, with Warren Buffett and Charlie Munger jamming all day. The "Woodstock of Capitalism," they call it.

Beryl Raff accompanied us to the meeting. Getting through the security hoops to our seats at the Qwest Center in Omaha was a bit cumbersome. I wasn't really sure why, until I realized where our seats were located. In front. The very front. As front as you can get and not be in Warren's face. "Guests of Warren." *He had a special seat for us.*

The four of us sat down, not really expecting to know anyone else there. Who else did Warren Buffett have *special seats* for? But as I looked around, I did recognize a few people. I looked at Jeff, and nodded for him to gaze to his right. I started humming the *Star Wars* theme song. George Lucus. Jeff turned back to me. OMG!

In front of us, Billie Jean King. And Glenn Close. Over there, Bill Gates.

At one point I looked through my camera at Jeff, with Warren Buffett and Bill Gates both in the background. Three entrepreneurs. Three philanthropists. Three of the richest men in the world (I just had to type that—a deposit for my dream bank). Fun photo for the CEO of a business built backwards. Most people cannot say they have been in the same frame with those two. This was getting a little "Forrest Gumpish."

OK. These were pretty good seats.

Warren was walking around in our section, chatting with *his guests.*

Beryl Raff told Jeff, "now is our chance!" She grabbed Jeff's arm and they quickly moved toward Warren. With 100 photographers snapping from the press box, all curious to know who the kid talking to Warren Buffett could possibly be, Beryl introduced the two entrepreneurs. Warren thanked Jeff for coming, and we shot our own photos. Jeff told Warren he had a gift for him, too, which would be delivered later.

Beryl then spotted Bill Gates and took Jeff to meet him as well. More photos. The press box was even more curious at that point, photographing the pair, *just in case this kid really was somebody.* (He is! He is the low vision, teenage philanthropic artist and entrepreneur, who paints GREAT ART! *Just keep saying it!*)

Warren Buffet occasionally auctions a "power lunch" with himself, for charitable fundraisers. Bidding has gone as high as $2 million for the opportunity to have a sit-down with him. I told Jeff his few minutes with Warren were worth about $67,234!

Jeff painted a very cool, abstract landscape which was delivered to Warren Buffett the following morning. Too many security hoops to give it to him personally. Titled *Along the Tracks*, it celebrated Berkshire Hathaway's recent acquisition of the Burlington Northern Santa Fe Railway (BNSF).

Back home in Kansas City, Jeff received a "thank you letter" from Warren, stating that the painting would hang in his home in Omaha. (GREAT ART in a prestigious place?) I believe the man could have just about any artist he wanted.

Generosity begets generosity, Warren.

The power of the hand-written note.

Along the Tracks, *44" x 28"*
acrylic on heavily textured
canvas, 2010. A thank you
gift to Mr. Buffett for his
generous invitation to join
his "A" list at the annual
Berkshire Hathaway shareholders
meeting in Omaha. Jeff only
smiled at Warren's ludicrous
offer to buy out Jeffrey Owen
Hanson LLC, on the spot, for
$3.6 billion.

CRAZY 'BOUT THE O

Commissioned by *theo eyewear* of Belgium, *Crazy 'bout the O* is a five canvas series specifically designed to decorate the *theo* booth at the SILMO Paris 2010 International Optics and Eyewear Exhibition. Jeff, at age 16, was given free rein to create the art work, as long as it included screaming *theo* colors and an "O" theme. *Theo* gave the canvases away to lucky customers during the show. We visited the *theo* glasses designer during a trip to Bruges, Belgium in 2010, and fell in love with this charming canalled city.

HORIZONS

Beyond Adversity

I lived in darkness for about a year and a half. From the beginning of 2005, when Jeff's vision really began to fail—before any treatment was initiated—I lived in darkness. The edge of night. No horizon in sight. Not then. My mood so sober—so blue. Every ophthalmology appointment revealing worsening visual acuity. Sitting there watching Jeff struggle to read a line or two on the eye chart. Darkness. I broke down and cried at one of those appointments. I couldn't control myself. I just burst out crying. Couldn't hold back. At age 11, Jeff just stared at me.

And throughout chemotherapy and radiation treatments, the darkness continued. Every smile, strained. Every laugh, pretend.

Until *Jeff's Bistro*.

From the time Jeff was two years old, he and I drove to Jennifer's salon for our haircuts. Jennifer cut both of us. My little buddy in his car seat, later growing into the front seat, always there with me. It was a guy's outing. Get a haircut, and then stop for a snack on the way home. Jennifer would cut Jeff first, then me. Once a month, for years. From 1995 to 2005, that's over one hundred haircuts.

One hundred trips to the barber.

And then one day, I drove it alone. My buddy not sitting beside me anymore. He didn't need a haircut. He didn't have hair anymore. He was in chemotherapy. Jeff stayed home with mom. It seemed so strange, so lonely, driving there by myself. The car was so empty, so quiet. After ten years of monthly haircuts. Driving it alone. I cried in the car driving there. In fact, I cried all the time.

This has been a ride—a seven year emotional ride. It is frightening to see just how low your spirits can go. Crying in the car on the way to work. I shed so many more tears than Jeff ever did. So fragile all the time—to music, church sermons, books, movies and the stories of others facing hardship.

2005. The Christmas of strained greetings and shallow emotions. Hairless Jeff, sitting by the tree, opening gifts. "Hava, Hava, Hava Blue Christmas," Elvis sang to me. Merry Christmas. There wasn't much "merry" about it.

I would sit and think about these things for hours. A hundred different trivial little anecdotes that meant nothing to those around me, but brought me to tears. Me, the ER doctor that should have been desensitized to everything medical—to tears. Very counterproductive to wallow in your misery this way. You enter an ever down-spiraling course into depression. Very self-destructive.

And the adversity wouldn't go away. With so much uncertainty in Jeff's visual and medical future, there was always the threat of new problems and complications. Genetic disorders like neurofibromatosis are forever.

Can you get past this? Emotionally? How do you get past this? Is there light at the end of the tunnel? Can you get past adversity when it really won't go away—not completely? Or can you learn to "live with it," and not go stir crazy?

We took it one day at a time. I am sure friends and neighbors looking in from the outside thought we were doing fine. But were we? What were we doing that made it appear that way?

Looking back, we **did** find our way through this. In fact, we've come a long way. But how did we find our way through this? To come out on the other side and still have our sanity? (OK, tenuous, but intact). Getting beyond adversity so we could focus forward again, instead of wallowing in the gloomy past?

Did Jeff turn all this around? Did his parents? By choice, or by luck? By wishes and dreams? By prayers? By God?

I see now what we did. Now, seven years later. I see the survival tactics that we employed—the defense mechanisms that came into play. For all three of us. Jeff, Julie and I each had our own methods. But not at a conscious level. We didn't **know** to do these things. It's just what we did. We stumbled onto these by accident. Just reflex self-defense. But it worked for us.

This wasn't planned. We never sat down and wrote a strategic plan to get through medical and emotional hardship. And we never consulted a professional to help us. A counselor probably could have told us these things. We never thought to consult one. This is just **what happened.** Defense mechanisms engaged to maintain our sanity, and lift our spirits.

But you must take an active role in this. These things won't just passively happen to you. Action is required on your part. We took action, too, but didn't realize what we were doing. **The risk of remaining passive in the midst of adversity is to become lost**

in self-pity. Emotionally disabled, you'll be walking down the pity path, never returning to any type of normalcy.

Here are four ways to combat your hardships. Four tactics to endure your adversity—your challenge—your CLOD. Four behaviors we unknowingly discovered that worked for us. Whether it be medical illness, addiction, financial problems, emotional disorders, personal disputes or divorce, these four steps offer you a plan to get beyond adversity.

It is not the challenge, but rather your **response** to the challenge that defines you. Here is a road map for your response.

Moving Beyond Adversity

1. LET'S FACE IT Face up to the problem. Openness. First to yourself. *My child is not normal. He is going blind. He has a brain tumor.* Admit it. No denial. And then, maybe more difficult, tell the world! Don't keep it a secret. Yes, you have a problem. You don't live in a perfect little world. This is no time to go private.

Why do people do this? Why do they feel they should keep major problems a secret? To spare the feelings of others? Too proud or perfect to have a problem? Self pride will defeat you. You need to confide in those around you—not for their pity, but so they can *help* you! (See support system below).

Do the obvious. Tell your family, your friends, your doctor, your counselor, your financial advisor, your creditors. Tell everyone who needs to know, who might be able to help and support you. Just face up to it!

And seek information. Research everything. Get it all out on the table. You can't make proper decisions without all the information.

Never easier to do than in the current electronic age. Get on the internet. Knowledge is a powerful tool to alleviate anxiety. The unknown is what frightens you. Know what you are up against, know your enemies, know your CLOD.

We could have kept Jeff's neurofibromatosis a secret. His learning disabilities, his ADHD, his low vision, his CLOD—all could have been concealed if we worked at it. Only those very close to us would ever know. But why? Do people around you really care? Will they think less of you? If so, we haven't noticed. And because of CLOD, a lot more blessings have come Jeff's way than any type of discrimination. Just fess up!

2. SUPPORT SYSTEM We all need one, even if we aren't dealing with hardship. And when the going gets tough, this is your safety net.

Family is the obvious first, but we didn't have the luxury *(what am I saying?)* of any relatives living close by. Jeff and his parents depended on friends and neighbors for emotional support. This was tremendously helpful. And our church and our spirituality contributed immensely to our mental well-being.

You need to rally your friends, your co-workers and neighbors. You need to talk things out (remember, *Let's face it*). Plan dinners, get-togethers and outings. Encourage people to pop in and out of your home. You need to keep talking to stay healthy. Let people help you run errands and go to appointments. They want to help. Give them a chance. Don't go this alone. Develop and use your support system.

3. DISTRACTIONS This is huge. This is the number one thing that got me through this—preventing me from being reduced to a sobbing heap of mush. We all used distractions to preserve our sanity.

Jeff started it. He painted note cards. Feverishly, he painted. And then came the *Bistro*. And then canvases, etc. Art, philanthropy and entrepreneurship. These activities distracted him. They occupied his mind so he didn't dwell on his medical condition and take the pity path.

Julie baked and baked for *Jeff's Bistro*. And then helped with note cards and charity auctions. During chemotherapy, she organized our neighborhood to adopt a homeless "Katrina family," gathering donations to equip an apartment for them. Julie began a regular exercise routine at a local gym, for a physical and mental vent, which resulted in a whole new circle of friends for support. And then came her role in Jeff's business and all the odd jobs it entailed—purchasing, accounting and being Jeff's chauffeur. Answering emails and organizing charity donations. Julie took on our church fundraiser the following year, procuring 1000 donations for auction. Endless distractions to keep her mind from dwelling on the 12-year-old with neurofibromatosis going blind from an optic glioma.

For me, it was Jeff's room. My major distraction was to remodel Jeff's bedroom. I apparently felt the need for a hands-on, physical activity to consume my idle time.

During 2005, Jeff moved from his childhood "train depot" room, to our guest room. It was larger, had a nicer bathroom and was closer to his parents. A security thing, I suppose. It was his choice. He was entering chemotherapy. And he was going blind.

But the guest room was pitiful. Especially for a soon-to-be-teen-

It takes five coats of red to cover white. What's with that? I don't do tile work—I never took a class in that. We hired a professional to lay the bathroom floor. For safety reasons, black and white "high contrast" colors were chosen for the shower, to facilitate Jeff's low vision. Julie's cheesecake factory ran year round. She not only baked for the Bistro, but she also sold her baked goods to friends throughout the year, as a distraction.

age boy. He said it was decorated in "doily." He was right. I really couldn't believe he was moving in there. I would have stayed in the juvenile train room rather than *granny's lace and quilts*. But he moved—closer to his parents.

So a decision was made to remodel the room. Jeff wanted a sleek, contemporary, straight-lined, loft-style room. And I agreed. Me, ER doctor and carpenter.

The destruction/construction began in the fall of 2005, during chemotherapy. What Jeff thought was a temporary eviction, dragged on for eight months of total make-over. It consumed me, which was great! Jeff "camped" on our bedroom floor, or in our closet for the messiest parts of the demolition. But he supervised the construction process. Holes were cut in one wall to install glass blocks. Two chests of drawers were recessed into the dead space behind closet walls. The bathroom was gutted and replaced with a high-tech shower and sink. The room was rewired, replumbed, retiled, repainted, recarpeted and refurnished. And I was distracted. Totally distracted. The project saved my sanity.

The result—**stunning**—if I do say so myself, (pat on back, here) considering my medical school curriculum did not offer a "shop" class. And Jeff loved it. We all did. A great distraction. And we are still using distraction, to this day, to keep our minds and bodies busy, with our feet planted on the high road rather than the pity path.

4. HUMOR May not be easy for some. It is hard to laugh in the midst of adversity. I wasn't laughing. But you have to keep your head and keep your cool. You need to surround yourself with things that are positive and upbeat. Make a point to read funny books and watch

funny videos. I made the big mistake of attending a depressing movie during Christmas 2005. Cried like a baby. What we craved was laughter and smiles.

You need to openly make fun of your problem. This is difficult at first, but you need to laugh at your CLOD. And laugh at yourself. Keep a sense of humor. Nothing is sacred. Don't give your problem any respect or show any reverence.

Jeff named his tumor CLOD. Even that is humorous. A farewell balloon launch for your brain tumor? A tuxedo at radiation therapy? Calling your lemonade stand a "Bistro?" These are all funny things. Little ways to make light of your adversity.

Jeff was always afraid of clowns. He never thought they were funny. In fact, he thought they were creepy. (I hope the "clown community" doesn't come after me for this—just stating the facts). As Jeff got older, we joked about clowns, and his childhood fears. So for his 12th birthday, during chemotherapy, we had a surprise clown-themed birthday party for him, to tease him. Clowns came out of the woodwork to attend. It was hysterical, and Jeff loved it— right there in the midst of chemotherapy. Humor.

With these four techniques—**facing your problem, developing a support system, distractions and humor**—we survived. And we continue to use these methods to carry on day-to-day. They are ingrained now, and will forever be life skills that will carry us through whatever calamity or hardship may follow.

****

Springtime, 2006. Radiation just completed. Good-bye CLOD. Jeff's vision at its lowest point—our spirits at their lowest point.

Humor. Send in the clowns. Jeff still had hair for his 12th birthday.
Chemotherapy had just begun. But he soon needed a wig, and tried
several before choosing this one. Jeff and Wundy often dressed alike.
I took endless funny photos on vacations, like this peculiar tree growing
on the island of St. Kitts.

All of us emotionally drained.

Jeff finally moved into his newly remodeled bedroom. He loved it and was very proud of the result. **Distractions that get you past adversity.** Every design detail was Jeff's. We let him have free rein. Sounds risky, doesn't it? And what does a 12-year-old kid know about home decorating?

Well, it probably was a sign of things to come. I couldn't have known it at the time. I was still looking at a broken vase, surveying the damages.

Jeff sat on his new contemporary bed and announced, "All I need now is a really cool chair."

But our budget was a little stretched at the moment. I didn't want to disappoint him, but the chair would have to wait awhile. (*Yeah, well, you know the rest of the story*).

We didn't realize it at the time, but Jeff was now formulating the biggest seven-year-roller-coaster-**distraction** of our lives!

So, the story has come full circle. At that very moment we were crossing a line—the limit of our experience was about to expand. A pivotal moment. A new horizon was looming. Easy to see it now. The darkness was about to end. A new dawn. Crossing a line. A line you step across where one foot is on earth and the other one climbing into new territory where the sky is the limit. A new horizon.

A horizon leading you beyond adversity.

Beyond the Base Ment

Jeff's art studio is located in the unfinished basement of our home in Overland Park, Kansas. What started out as one canvas on the floor, in an isolated corner of the basement amongst Christmas wrapping paper and ribbons, has now taken over the entire 1600 square feet of space, with 20 canvases in production at once. From a single canvas done as a favor for his eye doctor, his business has evolved to multiple commissions for a variety of clients.

Jeff's art work has progressed through five phases. In the beginning, it was nothing more than **fun** "kid art" for the refrigerator. Like we all did. Then, out of necessity, as a **pastime** during chemotherapy and radiation, it was intentionally used to keep Jeff and his friends entertained and occupied. A "mental health" activity. **Philanthropy** followed, with sales of note cards blossoming into donations to Jeff's favorite charities. Jeff's art then transferred to canvas, and his philanthropic art accidently became a **business** for profit during his high school years. A backwards business. And now, at graduation, Jeff stands on the threshold of turning his art business into a **career**. It can't just be an after-school job for spending-money any more—

it needs to become a sustainable source of income and life-support. It needs to move beyond the basement.

Jeff does not plan to attend college at this time. College will always be there when he wants it. He has been fortunate to win college scholarships, awarded for his community service, that will pay for college expenses if he chooses.

And Jeff has no intention of attending art school. Not because he thinks his art skills are already so great. He just does not want to "mess with success" or be influenced by outside forces right now. His creative juices are flowing, and that needs to continue, uninhibited. (Don't tell Elton John, or Lady Gaga or The Beatles any musical "rules" of what kind of music to write. Just stand back and see what happens next!) Art school will always be there, too (if they will take him). Jeffrey Owen Hanson LLC is booming, and Jeff does not want to interrupt or derail his momentum with any other activity.

But can Jeffrey Owen Hanson LLC really become a sustainable business and support an art **career**? And a philanthropy **career**? This crazy, backwards, accidental, no-plan business?

Decisions had to be made.

We posed this question to Jeff's friend and business mentor, Harry S. Campbell. Harry is a senior executive who has been a past president of two Fortune 500 companies, co-owner of an award-winning small business, CEO/board member of an internet start-up and founding member of the industry-changing Wal-Mart/P&G Customer Team. Harry's new book, *Get-Real Leadership*, shows you how to generate wildly successful business results by fostering trust, respect, and compassion in your team.

Harry pointed out the following. Jeffrey Owen Hanson LLC has become wildly successful, against all odds, "because a unique, valued product cannot fail." That, coupled with a terrific story and associated philanthropy have created Jeff's success, despite his shortcomings.

But Harry also pointed out our next dilemma. *We have created a beast!* Jeffrey Owen Hanson LLC is a beast. A beast that started out as a cute little pet, hatched at the foot of our driveway, that has grown until it can barely turn around in our basement. And the beast is healthy. But a little grumpy. And we needed to decide its future.

(in flec´ tion point) a point in time when a business comes to a dramatic change, or huge turning point, either positive or negative.

Harry said we were at an *inflection point*. The beast was experiencing terrible growing pains. His head was rubbing on the ceiling of our basement. We could hear him banging around down there. A decision had to be made. We either must feed the beast, and let it out of the basement now, or we must slay the beast, drag its carcass up the basement stairs and bury it in our back yard.

Up to this point, Jeffrey Owen Hanson LLC had not been an expensive business to operate. With minimal barriers to business entry, free rent in the basement and no specialized equipment required, the business was up and running with virtually no start-up capital.

Feed the beast. What does that mean?

The beast was developing an appetite. A *Versace, Gucci, Prada*-palate appetite. An appetite for attorneys, contracts, new website design. Trademarks, copyrights, liability insurance. Graphic designers, videographers, photographers, marketing firms, advertising costs and consultants. *All of this because of a kid painting note cards at a lemonade stand?*

For Jeff, this meant he must sink some money into Jeffrey Owen Hanson LLC, take it up a few notches, elevate the brand and secure its future as a career-sustaining entity. **Feed the beast.** Commit to some major investments in the company. Sink or swim time! Time to finally "earn" his seemingly easy successes. Take the financial risk that entrepreneurs are supposed to take.

Or...he could kill the beast, quit art, and go find a "real job." Or college (a state of "jobless suspended animation").

Or...as a third option, maybe the beast would be content to suffer in the basement for a few more years, starving, never getting any bigger or better than he was right now, before he succumbed to old age.

Which is it? Feed, or slay? Or fade away?

None of us could let him go. We all loved the beast! The beast must be fed! Jeffrey Owen Hanson LLC needed some major capital investments. But all of us wanted to see it thrive. Jeff must feed the beast!

Not that we wanted the business physically out of our basement just yet. The convenience, cost savings and control of the work environment make a basement business pretty darn handy. *Stay in your basement as long as you can.* But we all wanted the business to become bigger and better. We wanted to feed the beast, and watch it grow. It needed to produce more revenue if it was to support Jeff, his mother (and maybe his dad) with meaningful work and income. So how do we do that?

Harry Campbell immediately identified our main problem.

(**ca pac´ i ty**) the maximum output that can be expected from a person, a plant or company during a specific period.

We had a major bottleneck in our capacity.

Let's look at some numbers. Working full-time, even with his parent's help throughout the painting process, Jeff can only reasonably produce about 100 large (say approximately 30" x 40"), original, quality paintings per year. Exceeding that number only bogs down in repetition, lack of creativity and burn-out. Let's say the average sales price of a painting is $2,500. That means Jeff's maximum artwork capacity translates into about $250,000 per year, gross receipts. After overhead, taxes, more taxes and commissions, he will be lucky to pull down $100,000. Now that sounds pretty good for an 18-year-old, until you consider his business is in his parent's house and he pays no rent for commercial space. That can't last forever. Try to rent 1600 square feet of space and see what you have to pay. Even for warehouse space.

Jeff had no room for financial growth. He was operating at maximum capacity. Jeff was the bottleneck. The only way to increase income was to paint faster, paint more, and lose quality. Or raise his prices. Or diversify his products. Sell something else besides original art, that wasn't dependent on Jeff for every single product sold. Products from the business that expanded "beyond the basement."

It's not just about profits, either. Jeff's business was built on a philanthropy-first model. He wanted to continue generating substantial amounts of money for charity. And he wanted those gifts to increase, also. Increasing philanthropic gifts indicates the health and strength of the business overall. In order to accomplish that, the for-profit side of the business needed to be healthy, and expanding.

Jeff's prices had been climbing, but there is a limit to what one can charge, a limit to the value of your unique, valued product.

Jumbo art. Many canvases no longer fit in our basement. Jeff poses with cousin Heather and mom Julie in our foyer, as they paint background colors on a giant canvas that wouldn't negotiate our basement stairs. Our guest bedroom became a satellite studio in 2011, for this oversized canvas strung with wires. This isn't what I meant by beyond the basement.

You can push the bubble, listen to your customers, watch your sales and find your limit, which Jeff had done for the moment. Jeff needed to do something else, to get beyond the basement. Jeff needed to diversify.

For years, Jeff sold printed note cards, calendars and note pads featuring his art. Those **were** projects that went beyond the basement. But all proceeds from those paper products went to charity. There was also the reusable shopping bag for WHOLE FOODS, that benefitted Make-A-Wish. But everything **for profit** in the business required Jeff's time in the basement.

We looked extensively at canvas reproductions. Prints. Giclee's (inkjets on canvas). A way to mass-produce Jeff's paintings, to increase revenue without having to stay in the basement. Let a print shop do it. But they were disappointing. Very disappointing. They just were not the real deal. Jeff's canvases are extremely three-dimensional. Very chunky texture and thick globs of paint. You can't reproduce that on a two-dimensional medium. Jeff wanted to keep his art work original and very "high end." We did not see how we could market prints or giclee's successfully. They lessened the brand dramatically. Reproductions were not the solution.

Licensure. This is where we stand, on the threshold of 2013. Jeff and his mother are researching his art on high-end items. Women's scarves. Fabrics. Rugs. Men's bow-ties and cummerbunds. Taking his art business beyond the basement.

Inspirational speaking engagements. Ever since appearing in *People* magazine, Jeff has been approached to provide live motivational keynotes to corporate events. A presentation is now in production, to be available in 2013. This unforeseen "product" of Jeffrey Owen

Hanson LLC is the most creative one, only possible because Jeff has a great STORY. And it takes him far away from the basement. It is reproducible. And Jeff is no longer the bottleneck.

High-end paper products. This is one opportunity Jeff is exploring. These would include special edition, hand-painted note cards (like if you need to drop a line to Warren or Elton—**the power of the hand-written note**) on fine paper. Jeff's art work on these products would be out-sourced, far away from our basement, but sold for profit.

Fashion. A new horizon. Just when we thought Jeffrey Owen Hanson LLC was catching up on commissions and fundraisers, a whole new opportunity has arisen.

Fashion Institute Midwest is a non-profit that is committed to nurturing aspiring fashion designer talent. Their vision is to provide regional fashion designers with creative inspiration, training opportunities, resources and business incubation to unlock their creative entrepreneurial potential. Their "Omaha Fashion Week" is a biannual runway fashion experience that provides a professional platform to showcase the work of regional independent fashion designers. It is part show, part business incubator, helping designers produce and market their creative work.

Founders Nick and Brook Hudson caught wind of Jeff's art and philanthropy and contacted Jeff with an invitation. "Apply your art work to fashion, specifically women's dresses, and let's put it on the fashion runway, in Omaha, in August 2012."

Now this was definitely getting out of the basement. But a totally different concept and medium than Jeff and his parents had ever considered. DIVERSIFY! Originally designed dresses, hand-painted with Jeff's art work, fitted for models in Omaha and sent down

We all participated in the tedious process of copying Jeff's art onto fabric. These "wearable canvases" are one-of-a-kind works of art, with chunky paint in the Jeff Hanson style. Jeff fully intends to see one of his hand-painted gowns on the red carpet one day. I won't question or doubt Jeff's dreams anymore. I'll just wait for it to happen, and I will be standing there with my camera. It's in my dream bank.

*Jeff and Iowa State University apparel design student, Caine Westergard, hit the Omaha Fashion
Week runway. I sat in the audience and watched, in almost disbelief, as the crowd roared.
Pinch self. Never, in my wildest dreams! I have absolutely no idea how I got here or where this is headed.
I'm an ER doctor…with an art business…and now this? I swear, it was just a lemonade stand…*

the fashion runway? Can Jeff do this? And what do we do with the dresses after that? Is there a market for Jeff's art on fashion? Can they be reproduced—mass produced?

Jeff went for it! We all did. A three week interruption from the artwork in progress downstairs. Jeff linked up with an acquaintance, Caine, who was a student in apparel design. She created three original "generic" dresses for Jeff to use as a "canvas" for his art. Three of Jeff's previous paintings were chosen to be applied to the fabric. With hesitation, we all participated in the tedious process, getting the paint to go where it belonged, and safely protecting areas of each dress that were to remain paint-free. The art was copied to the one-of-a-kind dresses. Zero tolerance for mistakes. But the results were much better than any of us anticipated.

The runway at Omaha Fashion Week is 270 feet long. Attendance runs around 3000 people on Saturday night. We had no idea this would be this big of a deal.

Jeff's art paraded down the runway, "one painting at a time," and received very positive response from the crowd. Jeff and Caine followed, with Jeff wearing a tuxedo with cummerbund and bow-tie matching one of the formal dresses. It was a big hit, and a thrill for these two creative forces. Jeff on the fashion runway? This might take some getting used to.

Next stop? A "collection" of eight coordinating garments will hit the Omaha Fashion Week runway in March, 2013. Who knows where this will lead. Certainly beyond the basement.

****

Moving beyond the basement is not without its struggles. Jeffrey Owen Hanson LLC has many ongoing questions and concerns. Decisions have to be made, especially regarding marketing.

The biggest decision revolves around displaying Jeff's art in galleries. Ask any gallery owner, and they will tell you that an artist must "hang" in a gallery, for status and credibility. But they take a 50% commission for that exposure, and never have to wash the brushes. That takes most of the profit out of Jeff's work. And he is trying to pass some of his profits onto charity. Jeff has tried galleries, but is not currently in one. As long as his art work is virtually "sold out," he is resisting the gallery trend. But the day is probably coming, especially if his GREAT ART is to receive national exposure.

Another struggle is whether to continue painting commissioned works. This has been profitable, but stressful. It is not always possible to capture a client's artistic desires onto canvas. Or the client requests something that sounds awful—and then Jeff has to paint it and sign his name to it. There it hangs, forever, although Jeff would never have painted it were it not for the money. Is this the right thing to do?

Better might be to create "canvas collections" of approximately 25 paintings, released three or four times a year, at fundraiser events. *Important, new works!* No more commissions. Jeff would be "driving" the art, not the client. We are not sure which is better. Currently Jeff paints both "for fun" and commissions. Jeff loves totally abstract works. But the majority of clients prefer landscapes—even Jeff's abstract landscapes. Does Jeff paint what he likes, or "follow the money?" Follow your passion, or be a mercenary? It's a hard decision.

LLC vs. S Corporation vs. 501(c)3. This is probably the next step, to legally reorganize Jeff's business. There would be tax advantages for Jeff to switch to an S Corp. And his philanthropy opens the door to becoming an employee (maybe all three of us) of a non-profit. But more attorney's fees come with legal reorganization. Just another *Cartier*-snack for beastie. Feed the beast.

The beast still physically sleeps in our basement. For now. But Jeff takes him out for walks every day. Sometimes they jog. In matching tuxedos. But the day is probably coming when Jeff will have to buy "beastie" a bigger house. Already Jeff is painting commissions that won't fit in our basement. They won't turn the corner down the stairs. Jeff has to create the paintings in our unheated, non-airconditioned garage. That is occurring more frequently, and our cars now live in the driveway. This is getting crazy.

Just another sign that Jeffrey Owen Hanson LLC is moving beyond the basement.

CANYON DRIVE

Notice where the cars are parked? Uh huh. *Canyon Drive* is Jeff's largest work to date, as of February 2013. Spanning 20 feet, the five canvas masterpiece is an explosion of color (yes, including purple) commissioned for a private residence. Thank God it was completed before winter arrived in Kansas City. I was astounded when I saw it hung, and equally thrilled that I could have my garage back (at least for the moment).

LESSONS

Lessons Learned

I always loved a textbook that included a summary at the end of each chapter. Sometimes I just needed things spelled out for me, so I really "got it."

Living Jeff's journey with him, and reflecting on all the events of the past seven years, allows me to draw some conclusions about getting through adversity. And living life. You've read it already throughout this book, but here it is in plain English.

1. *(Do I even need to say this again?)* **We all face challenges. It is not the challenge, but rather your response to the challenge that defines you.** Do you believe this? No matter what life throws at you? We do.

We have a dear friend, Karl, who suffers from multiple myeloma, coronary artery disease and macular degeneration with vision loss. Yet to talk to him, he is jovial, interested in others and full of unconditional positive regard. You would never know he has several serious medical problems. Because he has chosen to NOT let them define him. I don't even think of him as a sick person. His **response** to the medical challenge is to totally down-play his illness, and move on.

He leads a multiple myeloma support group. And his life is filled with a hundred other things that occupy his mind, his conversation and daily routine. You can choose to do this—to redefine yourself in a positive way and not wallow in self-pity. It's your choice.

Don't let your CLOD define you!

American author and poet Maya Angelou put it this way. "You may not control all the events that happen to you, but you can decide not to be reduced by them."

2. **Generosity begets generosity.** *(You knew this was coming next).* I never realized there was a domino effect with generous giving. But we have seen it over and over again. Generous acts encourage others to become generous as well. *Jeff's Bistro* showed us countless examples. Jeff's generosity brought out the best in people's philanthropic spirit.

Movie director, actor and screen writer Harold Ramis (*Ghostbusters, Stripes, Caddyshack, Ground Hog Day, Analyze This* and many others) sits on the board of the Children's Tumor Foundation. He learned of Jeff's generosity to the Foundation in 2008, and invited Jeff to spend two days on the movie set of *The Year One*. Jeff went through costume and make-up, and was transformed into a "Jesus-appearing" extra on the set in Shreveport. Jeff is there somewhere in a crowd scene, with a cast of hundreds. We spent two hysterical days with Jack Black, Michael Cera, Olivia Wilde, June Diane Raphael, and of course, Harold. A very memorable experience, all because a very generous man was touched by a very generous boy.

Elton John said to Jeff, "If you give to the world, the world will give back." A generous act will eventually bounce back to you.

Jeff and friend Karl, in Jeff's studio. Karl is, himself, an accomplished painter, and showed Jeff a few techniques. On the movie set of The Year One, Jeff gifted director Harold Ramis with a canvas titled The Year Zero. Who wouldn't have fun spending two days with Jack Black and Olivia Wilde?

3. Focus on what you can do, not what you can't do. It's back to the self-pity thing again. OK, you can't play sports, you can't roller skate, you'll never drive a car, you won't be a brain surgeon. You can dwell on that all you want, feel sorry for yourself and make everyone around you miserable, too. *Don't let anyone ever forget it! Through eternity!* I love the gravestone that reads, "I told you I was sick!"

Or, you can "buck up" and find a new niche. Find activities or careers that interest you. Look for **solutions** to problems, instead of ways to perpetuate the problems. As an ER doctor, I am astounded by how many people consider themselves **disabled** by their medical problems. Life stops for them. And they are content to just let that happen. To let nothing more productive come from their lives. They focus on their **disability** rather than their **ability**.

Get creative! Focus on your passion. Find something to do! Don't make me have to come over there and find it for you!

4. It is far better to give than to receive. Sir Winston Churchill, Prime Minister of the United Kingdom during the Second World War said, "We make a living by what we get. We make a life by what we give."

Jeff loves those words. So do Julie and I. So did all the attendees of *Jeff's Bistro*, and the 101 Prudential Spirit of Community Award winners. What seemed like silly, hollow words as a child, have finally become internalized. Jeff has made many high-profile friends, simply because of his generosity.

5. Life has a few defining moments. Pivotal moments. Fork in the road, life changing moments. Events that can change everything, that will require a decision on your part. The diagnosis of your

CLOD. Choosing your response to a challenge. A balloon launch. A chair landing in your driveway. Meeting Elton John.

Or how about choosing your spouse, or your career. Getting a letter of acceptance into medical school. Defining moments.

Try to recognize your defining moments and carefully choose your path.

6. **Be passionate in what you do**. Harry Campbell told us, "Fanatical optimism wins!" Jeffrey Owen Hanson LLC beat the odds with the development of a wildly successful art business, built backwards, during a recession. Jeff defeated CLOD with humor, creativity, drive, forward thinking and attitude. It's all about passion. Be passionate in what you do.

Again quoting poet Maya Angelou, "You can only become truly accomplished at **something you love.** Don't make money your goal. Instead, pursue the things you love doing and then **do them so well that people can't take their eyes off of you.**" That's exactly what Jeff did. And then came *People, CNN, The Huffington Post…*they all wanted to know his STORY. They couldn't stop looking at him.

Steve Jobs said, "I have looked in the mirror every morning and asked myself, 'If today were the last day of my life, would I want to do what I am about to do today?'" We all have our occasional "no's." But if you don't ever respond "yes," something's missing. Find your passion.

7. **Never close your "dream bank" account.** Especially for your child. You've learned what I did. I didn't have any more dreams. Overdrawn. But without dreams for yourself and your family, you lose all purpose. Never quit dreaming. Never give up hope. Never empty your dream bank. I never will again.

8. Be a "Go-Giver," not a "Go-Getter." I can't say it as eloquently as Bob Burg and John David Mann. You need to read *The Go-Giver.*

9. Julie's three rules of successful parenting: happy, independent and giving back to the world. Create an environment in your home that nurtures philanthropy and community service. Find the joy in helping others. In raising your children, if you have instilled these three attributes, you are an over-the-top parent. (We are still working on "independent").

10. Find a purpose. This book is about generosity and philanthropy. That became Jeff's purpose. And finding your way through adversity. Finding a productive outlet for your energy.

Philanthropy and giving back to the world can become very enriching purposes for your life. And remember, it is not necessarily about money. Your "giving" of time and talents are just as purposeful as cash. Jeff donates more canvases to charitable auctions, than he does cash to charity. It gives him great purpose to paint something and auction it to benefit others.

Rick Warren's *The Purpose Driven Life*, is filled with pearls to help you find God's purpose for you. "Knowing your purpose motivates your life. Purpose always produces **passion** *(which we all need, remember, from point number six above, **so that you do things so well that people can't take their eyes off you**)*. Nothing energizes like a clear purpose." Find your purpose. Find your passion.

Jeff Hanson now says he is living "The **Purple** Driven Life." It's tongue-in-cheek, implying that his **purpose** is to use art to change the world. So far, it's working. And as Jeff says, "the painting is not done until the purple goes on." *The **Purple** Driven Life.*

And, finally, though not really a lesson of life, I must emphasize that we not take ourselves too seriously. Humor helps every situation. Take the art community, for example. "Anger's Third Response?" Need I say more? We tease the art world a little (*OK, a lot*). But we need to laugh sometimes—especially at ourselves. Call art GREAT, and it is great! (*But important?*)

George Bernard Shaw asked, "Which painting in the National Gallery would I save if there were a fire?"

"The one nearest the door, of course!" Zzzzzzzzzzzt!

****

For the life of me, I could not have told you these ten things a year ago. Living this journey day-to-day totally obscured the life lessons. Too many emotions. Just a crazy roller coaster ride. I didn't even consider the fact that there might be some valuable lesson in any of it. Life was just leading me along. Only now, as I tell the story and try to draw some sensible conclusions from all of this, can I step back in a moment of clarity and put this to paper.

I asked Jeff what the past seven years have meant to him. Can he walk away from all of this and make any generalized statement about what he has learned?

I guess I was expecting something profound. Like Dorothy telling the Wizard she won't go searching over the rainbow anymore for something that was really right there in her own back yard all along.

But here is what Jeff said. He took it 180 degrees.

"Thank you, CLOD, for making it all happen."

Unconditional Positive Regard? Toward CLOD?

OK, then. Lesson Learned.

Lessons from CLOD.

TONGUES OF FIRE

Acts 2:1-12, "The Holy Spirit at Pentecost" was Jeff's inspiration for this painting. It was gifted to the United Methodist Church of the Resurrection West, in Olathe, KS, in 2011. The "white hot," 28" x 54" heavily textured acrylic on canvas depicts the descent of the Holy Spirit in the Christian season of Pentecost. Notice the addition of purple, a color of royalty, and ubiquitous to Jeff's wardrobe as well. The purple driven life.

Changing The World Through Art

Changing the world. Is that so important? Why do we care about this world? Why do we spend so much time and effort trying to improve this world and the people on it? Why don't we just selfishly look out for number one? Bury our head in the sand.

(world) the planet earth, a celestial body, and its inhabitants. Human society and the whole body of living persons. The concerns of the earth, and its affairs.

Let's take a look at ourselves from a different perspective.

In 1977, NASA launched the Voyager I spacecraft on a mission to survey the distant planets. Traveling past Jupiter in 1979, and Saturn in 1981, spectacular photographs were returned to earth. Much scientific information was gathered. But then Voyager left the plane of the solar system and ventured off into the dark unknown. Traveling at 40,000 miles per hour, it continues to this day, leaving our solar system forever. The farthest man-made object from Earth. Currently 11.3 billion miles away. We still receive weak signals from it, and send it commands, as it amazingly functions in frozen outer space, using only the technology of that era.

In 1981, astronomer Carl Sagan made a simple but noteworthy request of NASA. Have Voyager take one last picture of the planet Earth. Before it was too far gone. From its deep space vantage point. To see Earth amongst its planet neighbors. Its solar system family. From a distance.

The idea was discussed over a few years and was delayed because of some technical issues. But in 1990, at a distance of 3.7 billion miles, NASA commanded Voyager to turn its camera back towards Earth, and take the final family photo.

The photographic result was more astounding from a philosophical standpoint than a scientific one. The planet Earth was reduced to a "pale, blue dot."

On the photograph, Earth, in all of its arrogance through human history, was represented—not as a planet, not as a spot, not as a dot, not as a pixel—no, our home planet, home of the *Homo sapiens*, and current winner of the Golden Global Warming Award, was revealed to be a speck, 0.12 pixel in size!

OK, Jeff. Is this the world you want to change? Whoville?

I absolutely love Carl Sagan's analysis of the photo.

"From this distant vantage point, the Earth might not seem of any particular interest. But for us, it's different. Consider again that dot. That's here. That's home. That's us. On it everyone you love, everyone you know, everyone you ever heard of, every human being who ever was, lived out their lives. Every saint and sinner in the history of our species lived there—on a mote of dust suspended in a sunbeam."

"There is perhaps no better demonstration of the folly of human conceits than this distant image of our tiny world. **To me, it underscores our responsibility to deal more kindly with one another, and to preserve and cherish the pale blue dot, the only home we've ever known.**"

This is home, folks. Maybe not so significant in the big scope of things. But it's all we've got. And the people currently living here with us are our only family.

So how are you going to spend your limited time on the "dot?" How are you going to spend your "dash?"

My mom, Jeff's grandmother that he never met, Helen Louise Britson Hanson, lived from 1914-1981. You see that little hyphen between the years—that's mom's "dash." That tiny horizontal line represents everything that occurred in my mom's life, from her birth to her death. Stare at it for a second. The dash. Her childhood in Iowa, her high school graduation, the day she hit a deer with our old blue Plymouth, her marriage, her kids, her joys, her tears, her work, her play, her rheumatoid arthritis, her death, all there. In that dash. On her grave stone. I'm in there somewhere, too, on that little dash. Mom's dash. If you haven't read Linda Ellis' poem, "The Dash," you must.

Our planet reduced to a dot, our life reduced to a dash. Our existence, so trivial. Our quarrels, wars and differences seem to lose all relevance. Our STORY, all meaning.

So how do you want to spend your dash on the dot?

Do you like how your dash is going these days, on the dot?

Have you noticed our dot is getting sicker, and people's dashes are suffering?

Remember SOS, in Morse code? ...---... It's a distress signal.

Dot, dot, dot. Dash, dash, dash. Dot, dot, dot.

Maybe we should try to change the dot—the world. Maybe it would give our dash **purpose** to change the dot—the world. To extend the measure of who we can be.

We all have nonpartisan, for the common good, vested interest in preserving and improving the world and our cohabitants. This is our only dot. And our only dash. There won't be another. Whether for self-preservation and personal gain, religious calling and spiritual satisfaction, legacy, or need for giving back—all of us can find a reason to improve something in the world around us.

Elton John is changing the world through music. Money generated through his concerts and fundraisers support the Elton John AIDS Foundation around the world. He is saving lives. Increasing quality of life. To improve and lengthen the dash of children left orphaned to AIDS.

Tom's Shoes is changing the world by putting shoes on the feet of children around the world. No one should live their dash without shoes. Not on this dot.

Paul Newman through salad dressing.

The Prudential winners—101 ways.

Jeffrey Hanson through art. Changing the World Through Art. Adding purpose to his dash, on this dot. *(Color the world, Jeff! With "dot art?" Sorry, I just couldn't pass that up).*

Jeff is "changing the world through art" in three ways. His **art** obviously decorates and beautifies the world. His **philanthropy** benefits many people through his art donations to various charitable auctions. And his **entrepreneurship** employs others through his purchase of art supplies and resources to create his products.

Jeff believes, "every act of kindness helps create kinder communities, more compassionate nations and a better world for all...even one painting at a time." It changes our world, our dot.

****

This is the story of one kid. A story of what one, visually impaired kid from Kansas can do. A kid with contagious generosity, setting an example for individuals and corporations to become more philanthropic—to change our world.

A kid who responded to a challenge, and redefined himself.

Jeff Hanson's **art** is hanging in Warren Buffett's home.

In 2012, the Association of Fundraising Professionals (AFP) in our region named Jeff "Young **Philanthropist** of the Year."

In 2012, the U.S. Small Business Administration (SBA) named Jeff the Region VII "Young **Entrepreneur** of the Year."

The trifecta! Jeff Hanson is **defined** by art, philanthropy and entrepreneurship. Not the kid down the street who lost his vision to a brain tumor.

Jeff has a goal. $1M20! One million by 20. To raise one million dollars for charity before he is 20 years old. How cool is that? How many of us can say we did that? What great **purpose**. I smiled when I heard him say it on CNN, in August 2011. But it is going to happen. In 2013. Before his 20th birthday. ONE MILLION DOLLARS! Jeff's mom has been keeping careful record. (Type-A, remember?). We estimate Jeff's artwork will have generated one million dollars for various charitable foundations by September, 2013. The barometer already reads over $750,000 on Jeff's 19th birthday.

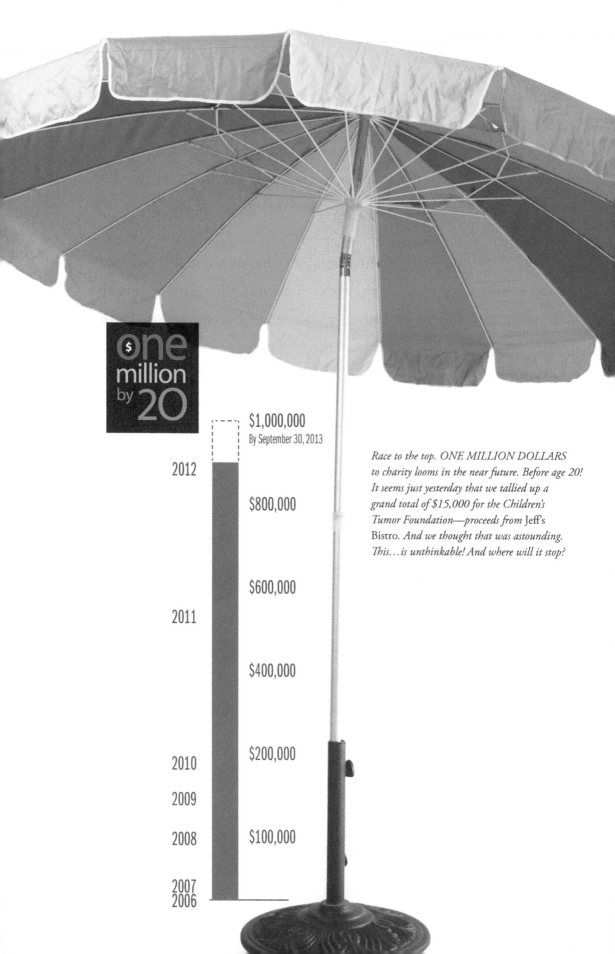

$one million by 20

$1,000,000
By September 30, 2013

2012

$800,000

$600,000

2011

$400,000

$200,000

2010

2009

$100,000

2008

2007
2006

Race to the top. ONE MILLION DOLLARS to charity looms in the near future. Before age 20! It seems just yesterday that we tallied up a grand total of $15,000 for the Children's Tumor Foundation—proceeds from Jeff's Bistro. And we thought that was astounding. This…is unthinkable! And where will it stop?

Get ready for a party! A media event. I feel it coming. Hey *CNN, People, USA Today, Huffington Post*! We'll be seeing you soon. You don't know it yet, but Jeff Hanson has a **passion** for philanthropy, and **he is doing it so well you won't be able to take your eyes off him!**

Why does Jeff want to change the world? This tiny, insignificant dot-dash world? This world you can barely find on a photograph taken from within our own galaxy?

Henry David Thoreau wrote, "It's not what you **look** at that matters—it's what you **see**."

Visually impaired Jeff Hanson said, "It's not how you **see** the world that matters, it's how you **change** the world." To give **purpose** to our dash on the dot.

And who is going to change the world?

I yield to Dr. Seuss, from *The Lorax*.

"Unless someone like you cares a whole awful lot, nothing is going to get better. IT'S NOT."

****

So, I end this where I began. Sitting on our back patio, gazing at a sky filled with stars. Voyager is probably looking toward me now, squinting his camera eye, tilting his analog brain, wondering whether he will ever return home—to the "pale, blue dot" now long out of his view. Will he really keep traveling for eternity?

I am now certainly in better spirits than I was seven years ago *(reread page 13, if you can bear it)*. Jeff and Julie are down in the basement, painting fabric for the next runway show. Who would have thought? That was never in my dream bank!

I told you Jeff had a great story. An over-the-top story. An emotional roller coaster of a story. Maybe the best story I've ever heard. (I'm not biased). You can't pack much more than this into seven years. Not to a 12-year-old kid from Kansas.

Now I finally know where all this was headed. At least through 2013. I can dream again. My dream bank is bulging with deposits. $1M20!?

And the journey continues, with a very exciting horizon. The beast has left the basement and Jeff has him on a leash, taking him for a walk. Sometimes a run. I'm not sure who is leading whom.

What is it about stars, anyway? Why do we ponder them so much? Light emitted eons ago, finally reaching my eyes on this tiny little planet, in my back yard. Every creature that has ever lived has gazed up at them and wondered what is out there. Everyone **Wishing Upon A Star.**

I never told you what happened to my old telescope that night. I packed it away and never looked through it again. I couldn't make myself. I love astronomy. It cost several hundred dollars. But it made me cry. **You can't see stars with tears in your eyes.** I think Julie sent it away to our church rummage sale one day when I wasn't home. Anyway, it's not in our house anymore.

I made a wish that night. A prayer. Now you've read what happened.

The Christian Apostle, Paul, while living and preaching in Ephesus, Turkey, wrote an amazing letter to the Corinth, Greece church in 54 A.D. I love *The Living Bible* translation of *I Corinthians 13:12*.

"In the same way, we can see and understand only a little about God now, as if we were peering at his reflection in a poor mirror; but someday we are going to see Him in his completeness, face to face. **Now all that I know is hazy and blurred**, but then I will see everything clearly, just as clearly as God sees into my heart right now."

Jeff will see that clearly someday, too.

But he already sees our world remarkably well, for a teenage kid with low vision. And his projects are changing the world. Projects like his driveway bistro.

Small things done with great love change the world.

Every act of kindness helps create kinder communities, more compassionate nations and a better world for all...even one painting at a time.

There never was another *Jeff's Bistro*. Not since that amazing, pivotal summer of 2006. We were constantly encouraged by friends and neighbors to recreate it. But a former school teacher of Jeff's advised to the contrary. She said if you go on a trip for a family vacation and have the time of your life, with incredible experiences and memories, *don't ever go there again!* Don't try to reproduce it. It will never be as good. The magic will be gone. Things won't be the same. You'll just keep comparing it to the past.

Better to savor your memories, don't try to relive them. Move on. Go someplace else. Create new memories. So that's what we did.

Jeff still has the fine Italian leather, Natuzzi recliner chair. I believe he will keep it his entire life. It sits proudly in his room, under a giant picture of a younger Jeff handing Sir Elton John a check. Jeff still invites everyone who visits to sit in it.

As for CLOD, he never returned. But we realize he is the reason for many of the extraordinary events that followed. For that, we give CLOD credit. Jeff sees about 20/80 through CLOD's charred remnants. Maybe Jeff should change the spelling now, to CLAUDE, like another famous artist Jeff loves.

And the vase? The vase is beautiful. Reassembled. Redefined. A purple, mosaic sculpture. An important, new work! World renowned. GREAT art! Museum class. And it has great purpose. Now 19 years old. You can't even tell it had a crack in it!

We all face challenges. It is not the challenge, but rather your response to the challenge that defines you. Choose your response carefully.

Star light, star bright
First star I see tonight
Wish I may, wish I might
Have the wish I wish tonight

Now many youthful things have gone
But not that star I wished upon
Childhood doesn't seem so far
When wishing on the evening star.

Count your lucky stars, Jeffrey Owen Hanson! Whether you can see them or not.

God has blessed you!

You've CHANGED THE WORLD THROUGH ART!

Love, Dad

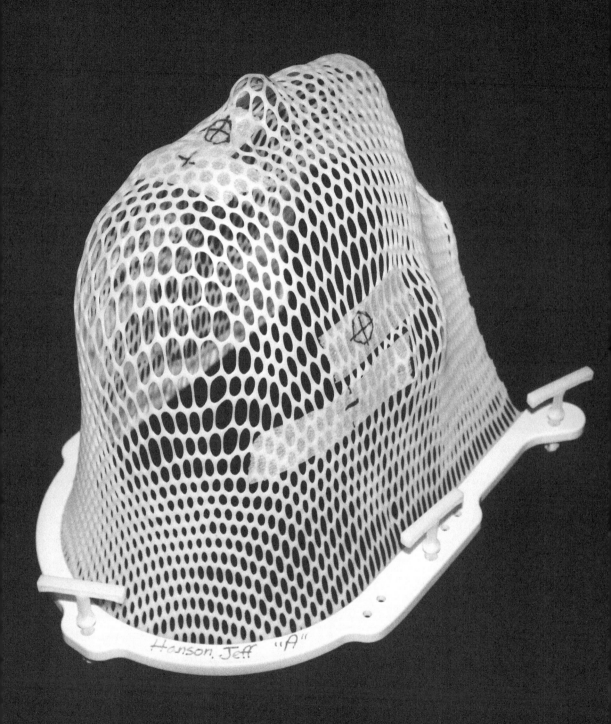

STARRY NIGHT

January 2013. Gifted to the Kansas City Young
Matrons' fundraiser, to benefit the homeless. Jeff
"saw stars" as he painted this canvas, depicting a
Kansas City nightscape. I look at it and smile now,
thinking back to that night on the patio with my
telescope. Tears. Tears of joy, now. But I wipe them
away, and we move on. You can't see stars with tears
in your eyes. And this is a new horizon.

Vase Artist: Susan Wiens

Two mosaic vases. The one on the right is gorgeous. I don't remember what I was whispering to the one on the left. Maybe…every act of kindness helps create kinder communities, more compassionate nations and a better world for all…even one painting at a time. And that's the end of my story…for now.

ACKNOWLEDGEMENTS

As sole author of *Lessons From CLOD*, I must also credit several others for their efforts to improve the content. To my manuscript readers, Kimberly Winter Stern, Maya Vance, Ann Thompson, and Steve Bedell—you will all find revisions as a result of your caring review. To readers Sandra Dusenbery and Rosalee Otta, my sisters who were able to gaze into my world and see what I could not, thank you for your suggestions and adding the family perspective. I carefully listened to all of you, weighed your comments and criticism, ran it past Teddy, and then typed what I sincerely believed was best.

To Pastor Adam Hamilton, Senior Pastor at the United Methodist Church of the Resurrection in Leawood, Kansas, thank you for your heartfelt suggestions. You will find yourself and your message between many of the pages, especially the last. It was you who first defined Jeff by generosity, in your book, *Enough*.

To Mike Rice, now friend and neighbor, who tipped the first domino in a million-long chain of giving, with a most generous act of kindness—a leather chair.

To Jennifer Bedell, Jeff's graphic designer at JJB Creative Design, thank you, thank you, thank you for your tireless effort and amazing book layout. You are family.

Thanks to Harry Campbell, close friend and business mentor, whose wildly contagious and animated enthusiasm for a young entrepreneur helped *build our business backwards.* The "Harry Sessions" were exhausting and entertaining. Thank you.

A special "shout out" to three talented photographers, Paul Versluis of Leawood, KS, (especially pages 96, 105, 139, 172, 196, 232 and 248), Herb Thompson of Omaha (Omaha Fashion Week, page 224) and Gary Rohman, Kansas City, (pages 174, and 212-214).

To Theodore Edward Bear, my silent companion, listener, sounding board and chief filter, who has final editorial control, thank you, *Wundy.*

And finally, Julie. You know, you are the gas pedal and I am the brakes. It was you who said, "Let's have a farewell balloon launch for CLOD," when a father cringed. It was you who encouraged Jeff to paint, when a father thought it juvenile. It was you who baked endless hours for a driveway bake sale, while a father worked in an ER. It was you who said Jeff needed a website, an LLC, a strategic business plan, a trademark for his signature, as a father stood back in hesitation and watched an art career unfold. And it was you who coordinated the endless stream of philanthropic endeavors, as a father applauded one million dollars by age 20. And now, Julie, it is you who I most thank, for teaching me how to respond to a challenge, focus on what I can do, and dream again. You put the stars back in Jeffrey's sky. And mine, too. I truly love you. Hal

ABOUT NEUROFIBROMATOSIS

Neurofibromatosis encompasses a set of distinct genetic disorders that cause tumors to grow along various types of nerves and, in addition, can affect the development of non-nervous tissues such as bones and skin. Neurofibromatosis causes tumors to grow anywhere on or in the body.

FACTS & STATISTICS

NF has been classified into three distinct types; NF1, NF2 and schwannomatosis. They are caused by different genes, located on different chromosomes.

- NF1 is the most common neurological disorder caused by a single gene; occuring in one in every 3,000 children born.

- NF2 is a rarer type, occurring in 1:25,000 people worldwide.

- While today there is no consensus, studies indicate that schwannomatosis occurs in 1:40,000 people, similar to NF2.

- The Neurofibromatoses are genetically-determined disorders which affect more than 2 million people worldwide; this makes NF more prevalent than cystic fibrosis, Duchenne muscular dystrophy, and Huntington's Disease combined.

- All forms of NF are autosomal dominant genetic disorders which can be inherited from a parent who has NF or may be the result of a new or "spontaneous mutation" (change) in the sperm or egg cell.

- Each child of an affected parent has a 50% chance of inheriting the gene and developing NF. The type of NF inherited by the child is always the same as that of the affected parent, although the severity of the manifestations may differ from person to person within a family.

- NF is worldwide in distribution, affects both sexes equally and has no particular racial, geographic or ethnic distribution. Therefore, NF can appear in any family.

▸ Although most cases of NF1 are mild to moderate, NF1 can lead to disfigurement; blindness; skeletal abnormalities; dermal, brain, and spinal tumors; loss of limbs; malignancies; and learning disabilities.

▸ NF1 also has a connection to developmental problems, especially learning disabilities, which are five times more common in the NF1 population than in the general population.

▸ The distinguishing feature of NF2 is tumors that grow on the eighth cranial nerve in both ears, commonly causing deafness and severe balance problems.

▸ NF2 brings on increased risk of other types of nervous system tumors as well.

▸ NF2 can also cause severe vision problems, including cataracts, retinal abnormalities and orbital tumors.

▸ Accordingly, NF research may benefit an additional 100 million Americans (i.e. 65 million with cancer and 35 million with learning disabilities).

▸ NF is not the "Elephant Man's Disease," although it was at one time believed to be. Scientists now believe that John Merrick, the so-called "Elephant Man," had Proteus Syndrome, an entirely different disorder.

▸ NF research began eighteen years ago by the Children's Tumor Foundation, and has been enormously productive ever since.

The following is information on Jeff Hanson's disorder, neurofibromatosis type 1. For information on NF2 and Schwannomatosis, consult the Children's Tumor Foundation website www.ctf.org.

DIAGNOSIS OF NF1

Neurofibromas, the most common tumors in NF, are benign growths which typically develop on or just underneath the surface of the skin but may also occur in deeper areas of the body. Neurofibromas, which are composed of tissue from the nervous system (neuro) and fibrous tissue (fibroma), usually develop around puberty although they may appear at any age. The tumors are not contagious. Nodule-like surface tumors are known as dermal neurofibromas. Plexiform neurofibromas grow diffusely under the skin surface or in deeper areas of the body.

The presence of multiple neurofibromas is an important diagnostic sign of NF. Single neurofibromas may occasionally occur in people who do not have NF. The number of neurofibromas varies widely among affected individuals from only a few to thousands. There is no way at present to predict how many neurofibromas a person will develop. Dermal neurofibromas rarely, if ever, become cancerous. Such a change, called a malignant transformation, may occur, although very rarely, in plexiform tumors. Therefore, it is important that patients be in the care of an NF specialist. Some neurofibromas, depending on their location and size, can be removed surgically if they become painful or infected, or c osmetically troublesome. A new tumor sometimes appears where one has been removed, particularly if that tumor was not removed completely. There is no evidence that removal of growths will increase the rate of appearance of new growths, or can cause incompletely removed tumors to change from benign to cancerous.

Café-au-lait spots, the most common sign of NF, are the flat, pigmented spots on the skin, which are called by the French term for coffee (café) with milk (lait) because of their light tan color. In darker-skinned people, café-au-lait spots appear darker in color than surrounding skin. People with NF almost always have six or more café-au-lait spots. (Fewer café-au-lait spots may occur in people who do not have NF; in fact, about 10% of the general population has one or two café-au-lait spots). The size of the spots that identify NF varies from 1/4 inch (5 mm) in children and 3/4 inch (15 mm) in adults to several inches in diameter or larger. In general, with few exceptions, tumors are not more likely to appear where there are spots. Café-au-lait spots are usually present at birth in children who have NF or, generally, appear by two years of age. The number of spots may increase in childhood and occasionally later in life. The spots may be very light in color in infants and usually darken as the child gets older. Smaller pigmented spots, which may be difficult to distinguish from ordinary freckles, may also be present in people with NF. In those who do not have NF, freckling usually occurs in areas of skin exposed to sun. With NF, café-au-lait spots and freckling are present in other areas as well, including the armpit (axilla), where small spots are called axillary freckling, and the groin. Axillary freckling is not seen in every person with NF, but when present it is considered strong evidence of NF.

Iris nevi (also called Lisch nodules) are clumps of pigment in the colored part of the eye (iris). Iris nevi, which usually appear around puberty, can be distinguished from iris freckles (commonly seen in people without NF) by a simple and painless procedure called a slit-lamp examination, which is typically performed by an ophthalmologist. Iris nevi do not cause medical problems and do not affect vision. The presence of iris nevi can occasionally be helpful in confirming the diagnosis of NF.

How Do I Know I Have NF?

Only a knowledgeable physician can answer that question. In the language of experts, the tentative diagnostic criteria for NF1 are: NF1, formerly known as Von Recklinghausen neurofibromatosis is present in an individual with two or more of the following criteria, provided that no other disease accounts for the findings.

1. Family history of NF1

2. 6 or more light brown ("cafe-au-lait") spots on the skin

3. Presence of pea-sized bumps (neurofibromas) on the skin

4. Larger areas on the skin that look swollen (plexiform neurofibromas)

5. Freckling under the arms or in the groin area

6. Pigmented bumps on the eye's iris (Lisch nodules)

7. Skeletal abnormalities such as tibial dysplasia (bowing of the legs), or thinning of the shin bone

8. Tumor on the optic nerve that may interfere with vision

Laboratory tests are now available in most cases to determine whether a person has NF 1 and 2. Gene linkage testing is available for families with NF1 and NF2. Direct gene testing is currently available for NF1 and may be available in the near future for NF2. These tests may be used for presymptomatic diagnosis. To find out whether you qualify for such tests, consult your nearest NF clinic or center. Occasionally, the signs of NF are not easy to identify. For example, café-au-lait spots may be so pale that they are not noticeable in ordinary light. For this reason, members of families in which NF has occurred are often concerned about whether they may have the NF gene, even if they have no obvious signs of the disorder. An examination by a physician familiar with the signs of NF is the best way currently available to determine whether NF is present. Examination of the skin may be helped by use of an ultraviolet light (Wood's lamp) which can occasionally identify very light café-au-lait spot pigmentation and can also help to differentiate this from pigmentation due to fungal infections of the skin. An examination that reveals no signs of NF can be considered reassuring, since it is extremely rare for an individual to inherit the gene and to show no detectable sign of the disorder.

Variability of NF

NF is an extremely variable disorder. The severity of NF ranges from extremely mild cases in which the only signs of the disorder in adulthood may be multiple café-au-lait spots and a few dermal neurofibromas, to more severe cases in which one or more serious complications may develop. The complications of NF are discussed in the next section. There is no way to predict who will have a mild case and who will develop serious complications. The majority of people with NF (probably 60%) have mild forms of the disorder. Another 20% have correctable problems and another 20% have serious and persistent problems. Many of the serious problems in NF mentioned below are evident at birth or develop prior to adolescence. These may include congenital defects of the bone, scoliosis, optic glioma and neurological impairment leading to learning disability or mental retardation. People with NF who have reached adulthood without having these problems are unlikely to develop them.

Complications of NF1
Disfigurement.

NF1 can result in disfigurement in a number of ways. Skin neurofibromas may develop on the face or on exposed areas of the arms or legs. The larger and deeper plexiform neurofibromas may grow around the eye or eyelid, or affect growth of one side of the face. Scoliosis, or curvature of the spine (see below), can affect appearance when it is severe. Growths can occur around the nipple (periareolar neurofibromas) which may be distressing. Rarely, an overgrowth of skin or bone causes enlargement of an arm or leg.

In some people, the size or number of neurofibromas increases during puberty and pregnancy, reflecting a possible hormonal effect.

There is no evidence that diet, exercise or vitamins affect the growth of neurofibromas.

While disfigurement, and fear of disfigurement, are often major concerns for those with NF1, not everyone reacts the same way to complications that affect appearance. Some people find that café-au-lait spots or a minimum number of skin neurofibromas are hard to live with, while others are able to tolerate more severe involvement. Those who are upset by the problems of disfigurement often find support and discussion groups to be helpful. If surgery is desired, primarily to improve appearance, a plastic surgeon may be consulted to determine whether a particular tumor can be removed. Plexiform neurofibromas around the eye are often managed jointly by an eye (ophthalmic) surgeon and a plastic surgeon.

Scoliosis.

Lateral curvature of the spine, known as scoliosis, is common in NF1. In most cases it is mild. Scoliosis usually appears in early childhood. A child with scoliosis will need periodic spine X-rays and physical examinations to determine whether corrective measures are needed. In some cases, a brace may be used to prevent progression of the problem. More serious cases may require corrective surgery.

Learning Disabilities.
Learning disabilities, often first noticed when the child starts school, are specific problems with reading, writing and the use of numbers which occur in children who have normal intelligence. Learning disabilities are more common in children with NF1 than in other children, and may be associated with hyperactivity. A child suspected of having a learning disability can be evaluated by a psychologist, child neurologist or professional with special knowledge of this problem. Many school systems provide referrals to specialists in these fields.

Large Heads.
Children and adults with NF1 often have large head circumference, which usually does not indicate any significant medical problem. Very rarely, large head circumference results from hydrocephalus, a serious problem which may require surgery. Imaging of the brain with CT scan or MRI can help determine if head enlargement is serious or not. Head circumference in children with NF1 should be measured periodically.

Optic Gliomas.
An optic glioma is a tumor of the optic nerve (the nerve which controls vision). This tumor, which fortunately is uncommon, usually appears in childhood and is first noticed because of poor or failing vision or bulging of the eye. Children with NF1 should have routine eye examinations by an ophthalmologist, neurologist or physician familiar with this problem. Treatment for this condition includes surgery and radiation therapy.

Congenital Defects of Bone.
The variety of bone defects seen in NF1 are usually evident at birth. Most are uncommon. Defects can occur in almost any bone, but are seen most often in the skull and limbs. They include:

▶ Congenital absence of the orbital wall, the bone normally surrounding the eye. Its absence may cause slight bulging of the skin around the eye.

▸ Bowing of the leg bones below the knee (tibia or fibula). These bones may be thinner than normal and bowed. If a fracture occurs, healing may be slow or incomplete. Incomplete healing, called pseudarthrosis, may also affect the bones in the forearm (radius or ulna), but this occurs very rarely. This is a difficult problem, which requires the supervision of an orthopedic surgeon.

High Blood Pressure (Hypertension).
People with NF1 can have hypertension for reasons completely unrelated to NF1. However, two rare problems associated with NF1 may result in hypertension: renal artery stenosis (blockage of the artery to the kidney), and pheochromocytoma, a rare and usually benign tumor of the adrenal gland. Both of these problems are treatable. Because of these possible problems, it is important that routine physical exams for children and adults with NF1 include blood pressure checks.

Information provided from www.ctf.org

Children's
Tumor
Foundation™

Ending Neurofibromatosis Through Research

For more information on neurofibromatosis, including NF2 and Schwannomatosis, please contact:

Children's Tumor Foundation

95 Pine Street, 16th Floor, New York, NY 10005-1703

www.ctf.org • 1-800-323-7938

REFERENCES

Burg, Bob, and John David Mann. *The Go-Giver: A Little Story About a Powerful Business Idea.* New York: Portfolio, Penguin Group, 2007.

Campbell, Harry S. *Get-Real Leadership: A Practical Approach That Delivers Relationships, Respect and Results.* Charleston, SC: Harry S. Campbell, 2012.

Dewey, John. *Art as Experience.* New York: Penguin Group, 1934.

Ellis, Linda, and Mac Anderson. *The Dash: Making a Difference with Your Life.* Naperville, IL: Simple Truths, 2005

Hamilton, Adam. *Enough: Discovering Joy Through Simplicity and Generosity.* Nashville: Abingdon Press, 2009.

Isaacson, Walter. *Steve Jobs.* New York: Simon & Schuster, 2011.

Sagan, Carl. Pale *Blue Dot: A Vision of the Human Future in Space.* New York: Random House, 1994.

Seuss, Dr. (Theodor Seuss Geisel). *The Lorax.* New York: Random House, 1971.

Simmons, Annette. *The Story Factor: Secrets of Influence from the Art of Storytelling.* 2nd ed. New York: Basic Books, 2006.

Taylor, Kenneth N. *The Living Bible: Paraphrased.* Wheaton, IL: Tyndale House Publishers, 1971.

Warren, Rick. *The Purpose Driven Life: What on Earth am I Here For?* Grand Rapids, MI: Zondervan, 2002.

I ♥ you Dad

CPSIA information can be obtained at www.ICGtesting.com
Printed in the USA
LVOW020401010413

326939LV00002B/2/P